Goodbye To All That

GOODBYE TO ALL THAT

A Souvenir Of The Haughey Era

Photographs By DEREK SPEIRS

Words By GENE KERRIGAN

BLACKWATER PRESS

Editor
Anna O'Donovan

Design
Pat Pidgeon

Produced by Blackwater Press
8 Airton Road, Tallaght, Dublin 24.

ISBN 0 86121 374 2

This book is for

Edel, Kareena and Stephanie, Sean and Donal, Eric and Mark, Kate and David.

And for

Matthew, Camilla, Thomas and Patrick.

And for

Michael, Jeffrey, Richard, Ciana, Aoife and Elliot.

And for

Every other child who will one day have to answer the inevitable question
- Who was Charlie Haughey?

Introduction

THERE ARE SOME FOR WHOM THE LOSS of Charles Haughey as Taoiseach was a tragedy. There are others who walked with a lighter step as soon as he left Government Buildings.

He was a great man, say some.

He was a villain who damaged democracy, say others.

We subscribe to neither position. What follows is not a biography of Haughey; neither is it a political assessment of his years in power; it is not a listing of what we perceive to be his faults; nor a recitation of his virtues. It seeks, through a combination of words and pictures, of broad strokes and telling details, to show not just what happened but how things worked in the Haughey era.

When covering politicians we must admit to a certain bias. We feel no obligation to list their many wonderful professional and personal qualities. We can rely on their highly-paid press secretaries, media advisers and advertising agencies to do that. Politicians and their helpers construct an image which they attempt to sell to the electorate. In over a decade of covering Charlie Haughey and his contemporaries we believed our job was to try to show how those images are constructed. We tried to photograph and to report not just the images they were selling but the nuts and bolts behind those images.

In short: this is neither a celebration of Haughey's years in power, nor a condemnation. Just a peek inside the political mechanism. This is what we saw, this is what we photographed.

DEREK SPEIRS
GENE KERRIGAN

• *Charlie Haughey at his Dublin home in Kinsealy.*

Bright Shining Faces

THE BRIGHT, SHINING FACES WERE ABLAZE with victory. Back then, on 7 December 1979, many of them were unknown to us. They were the obscure backbenchers who for months had gathered in holes and corners, totting up figures, whispering coded messages to possible allies, reporting back on yet another possible vote lined up for Charlie.

The success of Fianna Fáil in the 1977 general election, sweeping in with a 20-seat majority, had left the party with a whole lot of backbenchers with little to do but worry about saving their seats at the next election. Losses in the 1979 local and European elections, followed by two disastrous Cork by-elections, shattered the party's confidence. Jack Lynch would have to go. It was a choice between the plodding Colley or the man with the hint of sulphur about him.

Jack Lynch's cabinet backed George Colley, sure that they had the giving of the leadership. If anyone heard the distant patter of feet of the backbenchers, scurrying back and forth under the floorboards of the corridors of power, they paid it no heed.

The Colley camp was over-confident and lackadaisical. Had they tried just that little bit harder and swung just four votes, they would have done it. The vote when it came was 44 to 38 in favour of Charles Haughey.

Since 1966 he had been waiting for this moment, the moment of having his photo taken as leader of the party, chief of the tribe, the spirit of the nation. His face glowed, his supporters crowded in to be closer to him, to ensure that they were in the photo.

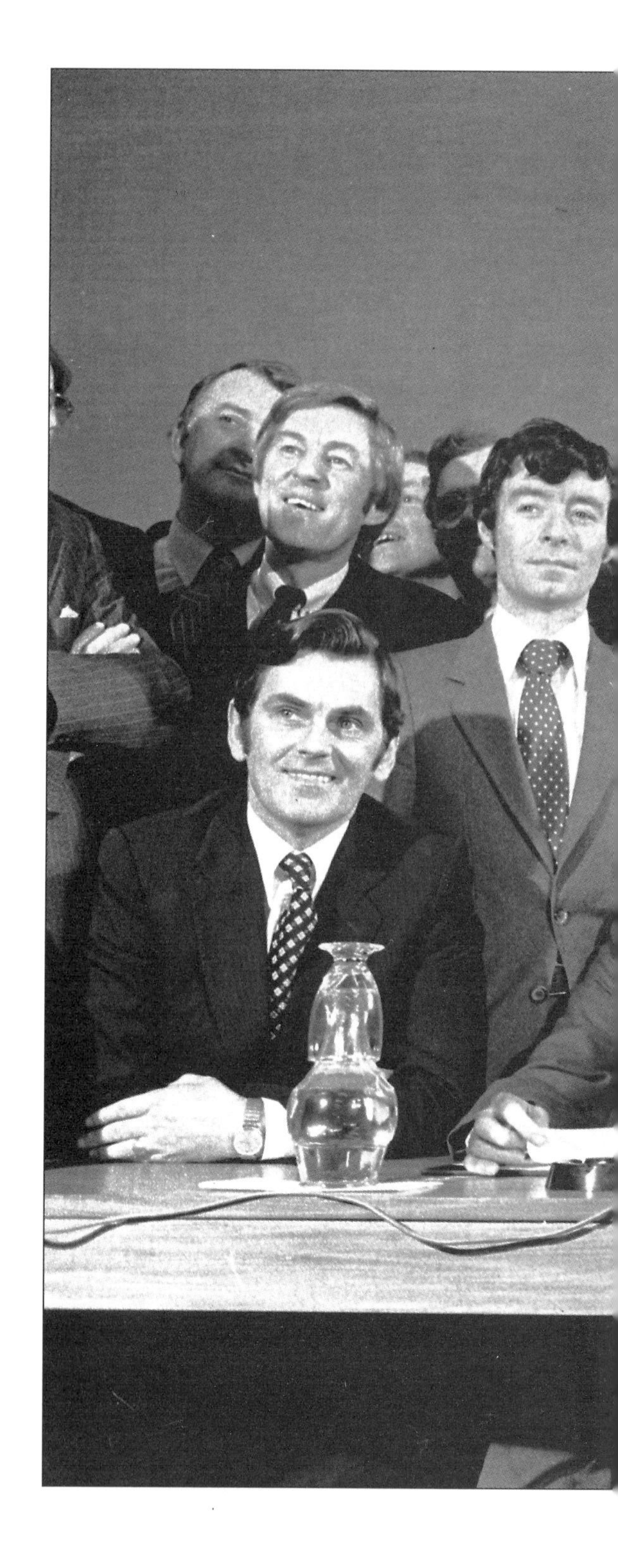

• *Haughey with his soldiers of destiny, minutes after being elected leader of Fianna Fáil, 7 December 1979.*

• *On the day they were first appointed to the cabinet, Ray Mc Sharry and Albert Reynolds kiss Mrs Sarah Haughey, the Taoiseach's mother.*

• *Haughey presents Sean Doherty, newly appointed Junior Minister for Justice, and future agent of his downfall, to the press.*

After 13 tumultuous years; the leadership whipped away from him in 1966; thrown out of office, arrested and put in a cell and sent for trial in 1970; the years as a backbencher, a has-been who might never be again; clawing his way back into the Cabinet, biding his time, creating photo opportunities and giving away free toothbrushes; after 13 frustrating years, the moment was here.

And his face glowed with the pride and the joy of that moment.

And behind him and around him his supporters glowed. Now he was where he rightfully belonged, now he would show them. Great things would happen.

• *Charlie Haughey and George Colley.*

The Myles na Gopaleen Era

"SOMETHING VERY WONDERFUL HAS already happened to me", said Charlie Haughey. "I've been promised, in a very sincere way, by George Colley, his total and fullest cooperation in my new task."

It wasn't true.

Shortly afterwards Colley made a speech in which he said that Haughey's supporters, in their treatment of Jack Lynch, "changed the traditional loyalty to, and support for, the elected leader". Colley would serve under Haughey, but he demanded a veto on the personnel chosen to fill the posts of Justice and Defence.

Colley's failure to win the leadership, and the deep disappointment of his circle, combined with the loathing many of them had for Haughey, set the agenda for the next decade.

You'd need an electronic microscope to spot the ideological difference between the two

• *Niall Andrews TD, at the centre of a storm of Haughey loyalists during the January 1983 heave against Haughey's leadership.*

camps, but the enmity between them was vicious.

Loyalty to the leader is expected in most modern political parties the world over. But only a functional loyalty is expected in most, enough to ensure that the party can get on with its job without constantly engaging in faction fighting. But disagreements, arguments, ideological clashes are expected and allowed for. For most modern political parties they are the very stuff of politics.

Not within Fianna Fáil. Until well into the

Haughey era the bizarre trappings of tribal politics would flourish. Without blushing, party members could describe themselves as "soldiers of destiny". They spoke with utter sincerity of their "great national movement". Usually, national movements are seen in nations suffering under colonisation. Decades after the British left the 26 counties Fianna Fáil spoke of itself not as a party exercising power but as the embodiment of an aspiration for national freedom.

(This might partly result from the fact that the national revolution was incomplete, in that the British writ still ran in the six counties. But whatever about occasional rhetorical exercises no one could seriously contemplate Fianna Fáil as a national movement dedicated to recovering the fourth green field.)

Charlie Haughey saw the party as "The Spirit of the Nation". The party summed up and represented the nation to itself. To be disloyal to the party was to be somehow less than truly Irish. To be disloyal to the leader was to be unpatriotic.

This strange tribal attitude to political loyalty is not peculiar to Fianna Fáil. Fine Gael, which comes from the same political roots, exhibits similar characteristics. Years later, when Alan Dukes was leader of Fine Gael, a front bencher would crack a joke about him. He said that if it was raining soup Dukes would have a fork. For this irreverence the joker was, with all the grim authoritarianism of an East European Stalinist outfit, driven out of the parliamentary party.

But it is within Fianna Fáil that the tribal rituals matter most. The Haughey faction's disloyalty to Lynch bred the Colley faction's disloyalty to Haughey. And from the beginning of his regime until he finally was driven out of the leadership, Haughey would always have internal enemies snapping at his heels. He would comment, in 1984: "I would instance a load of f..... whose throats I'd cut and push over the nearest cliff".

THE FIRST THING ON THE AGENDA WAS winning a popular mandate of his own. Throughout 1980, as Haughey sought just the right time to call a general election, if you wanted a road or a sports centre or an airport for your locality, you would never have a better time to touch Charlie's heart.

While this openness to regional needs might have been popular among the recipients of state largesse the media and Charlie's enemies were dancing up and down with annoyance. In January 1980, he had gone on TV to announce a new economic order. We were paying ourselves too much and borrowing too much and the budget deficit was far too high.

Haughey put aside such concerns while he played to the gallery in preparation for the coming general election. This ability to talk out of both sides of his mouth at the same time, to call for belt-tightening and at the same time ask everyone in sight what they were having, was a technique which Haughey would develop into something approaching an art.

HIS FIRST ARD FHEIS AS LEADER, FEBruary 1980. They cheered and cheered and it didn't matter if his speech tried so hard to please that it included everything and meant nothing. A peaceful solution in Northern Ireland, he solemnly told the faithful, was "our first political priority". Yet, he also told them, the issue of industrial relations was "so important that we will award it absolute priority".

The agricultural sector, he assured the

farmers who roared their support, was "still the most important".

With equal fervour he assured townies that it was the industrial sector "that we have to rely on in the main".

In such speeches, words didn't mean much. What mattered was the rhythm, the cadence, the nod to the party icons, the embracing of every sector as being the most important. The stroking mattered.

And the fact that Charlie had managed to hire the ITGWU brass band to play at the Ard Fheis. This was just a few weeks after the band had led 300,000 angry taxpayers through O'Connell Street, chanting condemnation of Haughey and his pomps and works. And now the union's trumpets and trombones pumped out "A Nation Once Again" as Charlie strode onstage.

• Smiles despite the republican protestors. But the effects of the hunger strike would cost Haughey the 1981 general election.

THE RUN-UP TO THE GENERAL ELECTION became tortuous. First the Stardust tragedy, which led to the cancelling of that year's Ard Fheis. Then the H Block hunger strike, which would eventually cost Fianna Fáil the election, when hunger strikers took seats that Charlie would otherwise have taken. As a matter of practical politics, it was important to try to squeeze the election in between any hunger striker deaths.

Even as the first press conference began in the party rooms on the fifth floor of Leinster House a rumour swept through those attending that Patsy O'Hara had just died. As it turned out, O'Hara had another five hours to live. But such events destabilised Haughey's campaign.

The lost election left him bereft. He sat on the front bench, often alone, day after day, waiting for the FitzGerald government to topple. It was like it was just plain unfair, that

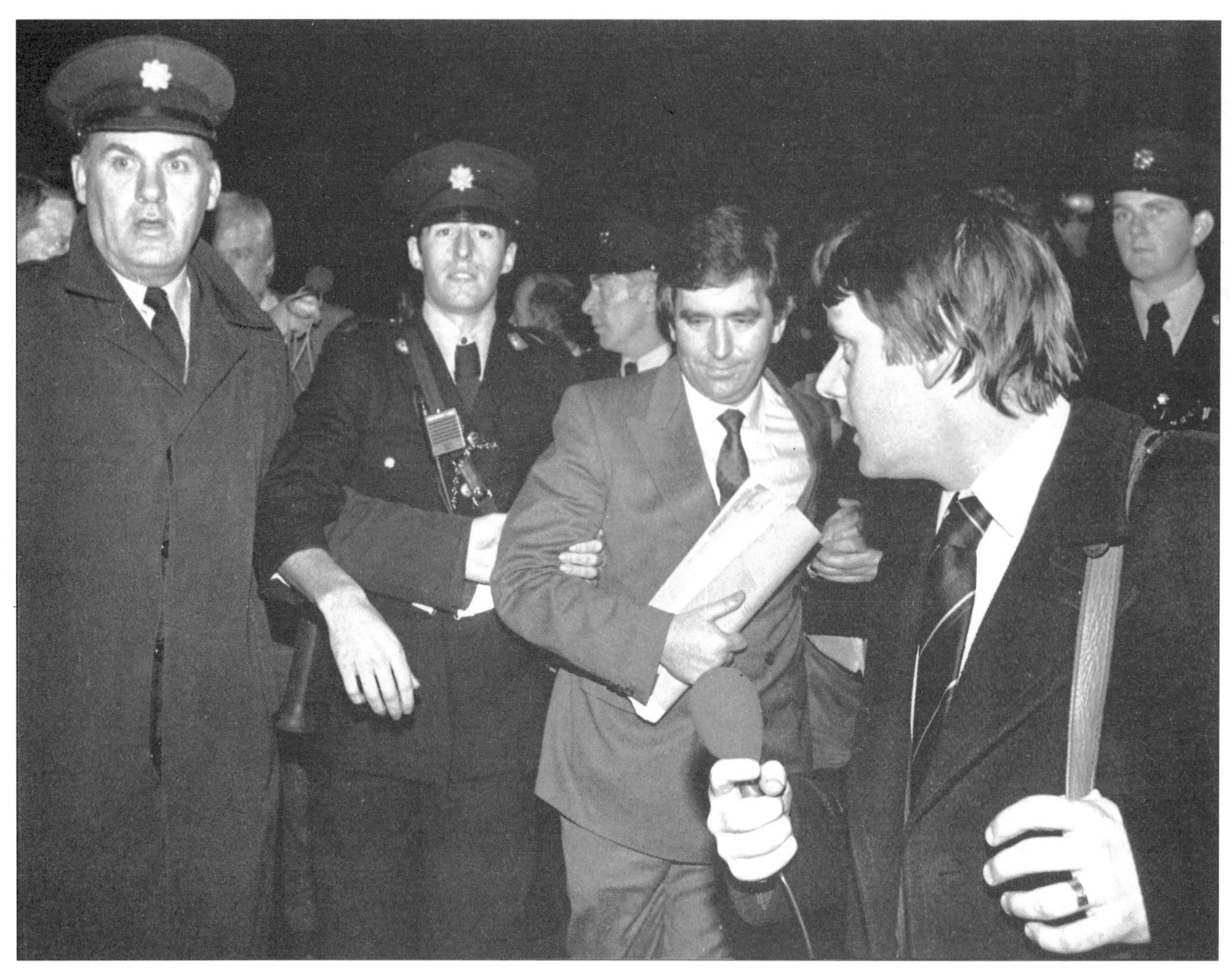

• October 1982. Gardaí escort dissident Charlie McCreevy TD from Leinster House as Haughey's fans howl for his blood. McCreevy had instigated the failed attempt to dislodge Haughey.

after all those years he barely had time to warm his Taoiseach's seat when they took it away from him.

When FitzGerald finally fell, after just seven months in office, Haughey couldn't achieve a majority in the ensuing general election, but he immediately did a deal with Dublin independent TD Tony Gregory, and in February 1982 he was restored to his rightful place.

It should have been the re-launch of the Haughey era after the false start of 1980, but fate was planning a special year for Charlie Haughey, one through which he would stumble wide-eyed, political explosions going off all around him.

Already, as though setting the tone of the year, Haughey's old friend Pat O'Connor was charged with double voting during the general election. O'Connor would beat the rap two months later, but the nickname "Pat O'Connor Pat O'Connor"would stick.

THE NIGHTMARE THAT WAS 1982 STARTED with the Colley faction pushing forward Dessie O'Malley as an alternative leader, after Haughey failed to win an overall majority in the election. The depth of the dissidents'

• *As Haughey he[illegible] [illegible]dership, passions flar[illegible] [illegible]unds of Leinster [illegible]*

• *Haughey emerges from Leinster House in triumph.*

loathi[illegible] [illegible]ey was exceeded only by the heig[illegible] [illegible]heir incompetence. The attempt co[illegible]psed and Haughey rubbed their noses in it, winning an endorsement of his leadership by acclamation.

That February victory was probably the last time for the next twelve months that Haughey felt things were going his way.

In April he drew the ire of opponents at home and abroad when he adopted a principled line on the Falklands conflict. He may have held the moral high ground, but they walloped him all the same.

In May, in what seemed like an ingenious stroke, Haughey reduced Fine Gael's Dáil representation by persuading Dick Burke to accept an EEC commissionership. Fianna Fáil annoyance that one of the spoils of power should be handed over to the enemy was somewhat abated by the fact that the party would undoubtedly win the subsequent by-election and thus a majority in the Dáil. They, of course, lost it. The goodie had been given away for no reason.

In June Haughey's government survived three Dáil votes only by grace of the Ceann Comhairle's casting vote. The year was only half over.

That same month Fine Gael's Jim Mitchell claimed that a phone system which Haughey had arranged to have installed in the Dáil had an "override" facility which allowed Haughey to listen in to others' calls. It was nonsense, with the existence of a technical facility being hyped beyond reason, but Haughey's reputation ensured that some of the mud would stick. In the meantime, a new phrase, "I suppose an override is out of the question?" was born. The joke was, of course, that while Haughey was being falsely accused of tapping phones, his Minister for Justice, Sean Doherty, was doing that very thing.

The succession of calamities, the surliness of the dissidents, the sense of siege within the Haughey regime, bred paranoia. Was British Intelligence behind it all?

The view of the party as The Spirit of the Nation meant that whoever was getting at Charlie weren't just anti-party, they were anti-national. The fact that the dissidents were leaking to the newspapers the details of the party's internal rows provoked Sean Doherty into ordering the tapping of journalists' phones in order to find out who was doing the leaking.

Haughey couldn't hear it, but the knife which would eventually sink between his shoulderblades was being ground and sharpened.

The incredible year continued. August brought a biggie. Malcom MacArthur, a wanted murderer, the subject of an intense garda hunt, was found living at Haughey's Attorney General's home. It was like God had gone on a long holiday and left Myles na Gopaleen in charge of affairs.

September brought a mysterious car crash in Kerry, involving Sean Doherty's ministerial car. There was no great scandal involved, but the secretive behaviour of those concerned created suspicion where none was justified.

In October the dissidents tried again, with Charlie McCreevy proposing a motion to get rid of Haughey. McCreevy wasn't part of the Colley begrudgery faction, but he joined forces with them when he lost patience with Haughey's inability to implement the economic policies which Haughey had professed.

Hardly had Haughey beaten off the second heave against his leadership, by 58 votes to 22, when in November he lost a confidence vote in the Dáil and his government collapsed. He lost the consequent general election and in January 1983 the new Fine Gael-led government triumphantly dug out of the files the evidence that Sean Doherty had bugged the phones of journalists Bruce Arnold and Geraldine Kennedy.

Doherty slouched off into the wilderness, carrying up his sleeve the knife for which he would someday find a use.

The dissidents tried again in February and were defeated again, 40-33. As conspirators they made Larry, Curly and Moe look efficient.

Haughey beat off the 33 stooges, but he was still out of office. After three miserable years of faction fighting, with election results ranging from awful to mediocre, a series of incredible events in 1982, his rightful throne had been swiped from him a second time. And now Haughey would be almost five years out of office, doggedly opposing every measure the government proposed. In short, the first eight years of the Haughey era were a disaster.

The pressures of that period accumulated. The mask of toughness cracked in 1983, when, under pressure at a New Ireland Forum meeting with Garret FitzGerald and Dick Spring, Haughey burst into tears.

• *Attorney General Patrick Connolly leaving Kinsealy following a discussion with Haughey after a murderer was found in his apartment.*

• *Journalists Geraldine Kennedy and Bruce Arnold read a government statement confirming that Sean Doherty tapped their phones. Peter Murtagh, the Irish Times journalist who broke the phone tap story, is in the centre.*

• *Mary O'Rourke welcomes Charlie Haughey, arriving by helicopter as usual.*

• *Heading for the "How much is that doggie in the window" stall, at St. Colman's, Rathdrum.*

Follow the Leader

THE REPORTERS STOOD SHIVERING IN the grounds of Charlie Haughey's home at Kinsealy, just after 7.30am on a bright and cold February morning in 1982. It was a Sunday, there was an election, so Charlie was doing the Masses. And the reporters went along to watch him doing it.

"Doing the Masses" is when a politician flits from church to church, arriving at each one just before the Mass ends, standing outside to greet the voters as they emerge.

A flunky came out of Haughey's Kinsealy mansion and remonstrated with an Australian TV crew. They had no business shooting film of the mansion, stop it or you all get thrown out.

Charlie emerged minutes later, a big smile on his face. He nodded to the reporters, stood there, and after a few awkward moments turned to one and asked, "Will you have a drink?" It wasn't yet 8am. It was hard to know if he was being ultra-hospitable, or satirising reporters' reputations for boozing. At times he seemed awkward in company and seemed to say the first thing that popped into his mind. The reporters declined the invitation.

Maureen Haughey emerged. "This", said Charlie, with a Biblical flourish, "is my wife, in whom I'm well pleased". Again, was he being funny, taking the mickey out of himself? It didn't seem so.

At one political event or another, such social awkwardnesses popped up again and again. Confident, even arrogant, he might be, and well capable of fighting his political corner. But Charlie Haughey was never as tough as he was made out. There was always a vulnerability close to the surface. He always had the capacity to do something slightly off-key.

Later that morning, during a filmed interview, when the Australian TV reporter insisted on asking him about the issue of contraception, Haughey would turn on his heel and walk away, the camera still rolling.

THE BUS CAME HURTLING UP ALONG the quay at New Ross, ablaze with posters and slogans, the loudspeakers urging one and all to "Rise And Follow Charlie!". A crowd of cheering kids surged forward as the bus stopped.

There was no Haughey inside, just a reporter from the Irish Press and a party hack. The bus had ploughed its way down the east coast, from village to village, all the time the loudspeakers throwing out to the cows and sheep in the nearby fields the musical invitation that they rise and follow Charlie. But, unlike other party leaders, Charlie seldom, if ever, travelled on the campaign bus. He raced ahead by car, or – preferably – by helicopter.

For the duration of the campaign, while fighting an overall strategic battle, party against party, the party leader must also lend himself to the constituencies for their own little battles. There are forty-one constituencies and each of them is fighting its own little election and the party leader, like a tribal chief of old, must come to lend his weight to the fight, deliver a nominal slash of the sword in the direction of the other shower.

The national party bureaucracy may decide

• *Padraig Flynn peels a stray election sticker from the sole of Charlie Haughey's shoe. East Galway by-election 1982.*

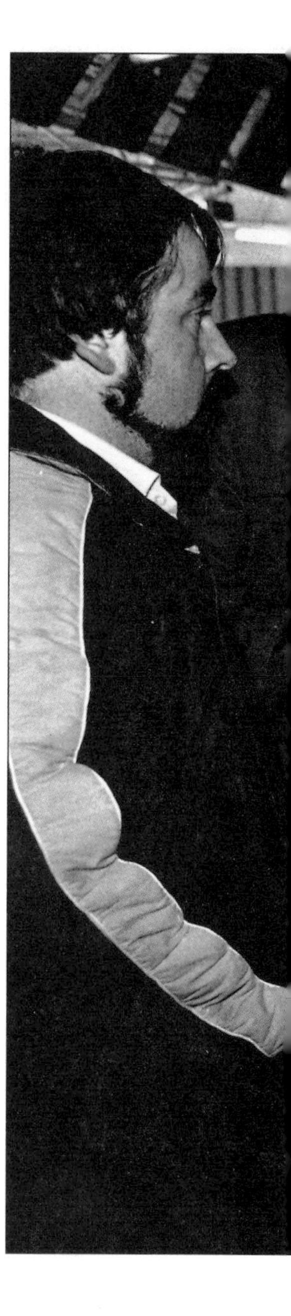

• *Even in supermarket queues there is no escaping politicians at election time.*

• *A moment of stillness in the hustle of the November 1982 general election campaign.*

• *I bring you my leader. Hugh Byrne TD, Wexford 1989.*

• *Doing the Masses. Brian Lenihan waiting to canvass.*

where the leader goes and when, but once having entered the constituency the leader becomes the property of the locals. He is taken by the arm and rushed from one event to another, party hacks and sympathisers are called forward to have their hands shaken, a kind of reward for the time they spend knocking on doors.

The local candidate benefits by being the one to bring the party leader to shake your

hand. At times on his outings Charlie Haughey was accompanied by a young man with a polaroid camera, who would snap a shot of Charlie with a voter and with a flourish give the picture to the voter to put on his or her mantlepiece.

Come election time you can't do your shopping without risking turning around to find a party leader at your elbow, in search of a mandate.

THEY WERE RAISING MONEY AT A FETE AT St Colman's, in Rathdrum, when Charlie Haughey came along looking for votes, one stop in a dozen made that day. There was nobody better than Charlie for making a splash in such a situation. He gave someone a pound for a raffle ticket and didn't bother taking the ticket. He moved from stall to stall, shaking hands. Suddenly there was a nurse standing in front of him, holding up a painting.

"I'll give you a hundred pounds for it", said generous Charlie, "And I'll present it to the hospital."

Nurse Katherine Keane paused and assessed her man. She stared Charlie in the eye. "Two hundred", she said.

The cameras were watching, biros were poised over notebooks. The politician and the nurse stared each other down. "Do I get anything off for cash?", asked Charlie. The nurse just smiled and kept on staring him down. It was the politician who broke, handing over £200 on the spot.

A woman came up waving tickets for her "How much is that doggie in the window" raffle. Six for 50p. Charlie had only tenners left. He gave one to her. A man selling raffle tickets was in like a shot. "Take one, Charlie, here y'are", he urged, and that cost Charlie another tenner. He quickly left the fête. Head down, plunging towards the exit.

Within a few minutes, his reputation for largesse, skilfully exploited, had cost him £221.

The Caravan

THEY ASKED THE OLD MAN: "DID YOU DO your duty?"

He said, "Yes, sure, I did."

This is Elphin, Roscommon, early afternoon on polling day November 1982.

There are two caravans outside the local school where the polling station is sited. One belongs to Fine Gael, the other to Fianna Fáil. Winter is coming in, it's windy and there's the odd spot of rain. There has been flooding in the area recently and it's not the best kind of weather for getting people out to vote but this is Sean Doherty country and here they always come out, 70 or even 75 percent turnout at every election.

The law says that the party workers can't hang around inside the polling station, so they wait out here in the caravans. There is no leafletting, no last minute solicitation of votes, just the caravans.

Some go straight home, but mostly the voters, having gone inside and made their choice, head for the Fianna Fáil caravan.

"Did you do your duty?"

"Aye, indeed."

Inside the caravan there are bottles of whiskey. Some men sit around glass in hand.

The old man comes along, he's using a walker. He is unable to step up into the caravan so he stands outside. He'd like a hot whiskey, the day that's in it. The hot whiskey is prepared in a glass. The old man waits.

The party workers, uneasy at the presence of a camera, joke and stall. The old man gets impatient. He's done his duty, now where's his whiskey? He has little time for, and perhaps little understanding of, the reticence of the party workers.

• *The old man gets his whiskey.*

He can't climb up into the caravan, they don't want to bring it out here where it can be photographed. Time goes by, the old man getting more browned off.

Eventually, after the party workers have had a little huddle inside the caravan, the whiskey is produced for the old man, having been poured from the glass into a cup.

A woman emerges from the polling station and is getting into a car. "Would you like something, Missus?", calls a party worker, holding up two fingers, indicating a small one. "No thanks", she says and goes off.

A few yards down the road the Fine Gaelers inside their caravan are making coffee.

Sean Doherty topped the poll in Roscommon.

• *Inside the caravan.*

• *The personation squad, Carraghroe polling station, Roscommon, November 1982.*

The Tally

IN THEORY YOU VOTE IN CONFIDENCE, the secrecy of the ballot box is sacred. In practice, information collated from decades of elections, general and local, helps the parties massage the vote. When you enter a polling station you are entering a party machine.

The parties try to have a "personation agent" sitting by every ballot box in the country. This aim is not usually achieved, but they come close enough. In many smaller polling stations Fianna Fáil is the only party which can manage to provide a personation agent.

The main function of a personation agent is not to guard against personation. It's true that if someone called Smith comes in and says his name is Jones and the personation agent knows him a breach of the law can be prevented. But such happenings are very rare.

When you vote, the official polling clerk, employed by the state, crosses out your name from his or her list. And at the same time calls out your name. The party personation agents draw a line through your name on their own copy of the electoral list. They are not usually identified as being from any party, they may appear to be officials of some kind.

At the end of polling day the party has a record of the names of everyone who voted - and in which box they voted.

Each box has a serial number. It contains perhaps 400 votes, sometimes as few as 250. That's the first part of the game.

WHEN THE DOORS OPEN AT A COUNT centre the party tallymen literally run to the count area. Some of them shuffle as fast as they can with their arms laden down with a personal computer.

We mostly hear of the tallymen through RTE. From early in the count and through the day reporters go on the air with the latest predictions from the tallymen. A somewhat romantic legend has been built up around these characters. Radio and television commentators speak of them in tones of awe. They are portrayed as people of intricate mind and mystical ability. To hear some talk one might imagine that, for instance, a Dublin tallyman need only hold a ballot box to his ear and shake it twice and he can calculate Bertie Ahern's first count vote and the probable destination of most of Tony Gregory's second preferences.

The prime function of tallymen (and some are women, but the same title applies) is not to delight us with early predictions. They are the party's shock troops in the fight to breach the secrecy of the ballot box and amass the kind of information which will help the parties manipulate the vote at future elections.

The tallymen run to the tables where the ballot boxes are being emptied. They will stand there all day, watching the votes being counted. They carry clipboards with printed forms attached.

The serial number of each box is noted. The clerks empty the boxes. They are not yet counting the votes for each candidate, they are just unfolding and stacking the voting papers. There is an understanding between the parties and the returning officers that the voting papers are unfolded and stacked face up.

The tallymen note the destination of each first preference, making marks on their tally sheets. By the time the voting papers are stacked, before a single vote from that box has been officially counted, the tallymen have a tally of the first preferences for each candidate.

As the count centre becomes crowded, some of the tallymen put party stickers on their backs, to quickly identify them to the party runners. The runners collect the tally sheets and bring them to the senior tallymen huddled at tables around the count centre. There, the votes in each box are compared with the votes from the same box at the previous election.

Of late, this kind of calculation has been computerised. Some party members have designed their own software (the Labour Party computer programme in Dublin South is labelled "A Product of Starry Plough Software"). This means that a keystroke or two can show the percentages for each candidate, in each box.

The computer programmes contain the data from previous elections and a few keystrokes can show the swing to and from each party in

• *The senior tallyman waits for the figures to be brought to him, as the count begins in the RDS.*

each box, going back years.

Older tallymen scorn such gimmicks and claim they can work it all out in their heads.

The tallymen are loyal party activists but at the count they are professionals and party rivals consult one another, comparing figures to ensure accurate results. As the count goes on the better tallymen can follow the distribution of second and third preferences with some accuracy, but the first preference tally is the most important.

The parties now have the precise first preference tally in each box. They also have, from the personation agents, a list of the names of the 300 or 400 people who voted in that box. They can identify precisely the way certain streets (in the city) or villages (in the country) have voted. They also have the names and the figures from that box going back over several elections.

In addition, they have decades of canvass information, from party workers knocking on doors. The response from each house is noted and over a period of years a profile of a street can be built up. This can be cross-checked against the tally information showing how that area voted. They now have information which can show the slightest shift within each pocket of voters in the country.

They cannot, of course, put a name to each vote, but they don't need to. The voting trend in each street, village or townland can be identified, providing a powerful electoral tool. The party knows which area it can ignore, which to massage. Ministerial favours can be carefully applied.

There are very practical applications of the information. At the next election, for instance, with perhaps two hours to go before the polls close, a local party hack may know that, for instance, 177 of the 224 people entitled to vote in a particular box have already done so. He learns this from the personation agents. He knows how many of the remaining 47 are dead, have emigrated or don't bother to vote. From previous tally figures and canvass notes, he will have an accurate assessment of how many and who among the remainder are likely to vote for the party. Cars can then be arranged to bring those people to the polling station.

Although all parties play this game it is Fianna Fáil which has the largest number of people collecting the information, the largest backlog of information, and the most professional approach to the job. The process provides the party with the information to support a real, practical manipulation of the vote within a constituency. It cannot guarantee success but it is a major factor in giving Fianna Fáil an edge against its rivals.

The process also has a role in emphasising the TD's powers.

One senior Fianna Fáil politician tells of an election in which the figures from one ballot box showed three votes more than he expected. His tallymen got on the job, carefully scrutinising all the available information. After two weeks they identified the three extra voters. This enabled the TD, when he next came across one or other of the three, to grasp the voter by the hand, look into the voter's eye, and say a heartfelt, "Thank you, I won't forget you."

Such demonstrations of the TDs apparent ability to look inside the voter's heart are worth a hundred party political broadcasts.

• *The computerised tally.*

• *After the tally is over.*

The Money Man

SOME OF THEM DIDN'T PARTICULARLY want to be there, but on the whole it's best not to turn down an invitation to lunch with the Taoiseach.

It was Thursday 8 June 1989, in the midst of a general election campaign. The invitation to lunch had nothing and everything to do with the election. Such lunches are a regular feature and the invitations had gone out a month previously, before the election was called.

The lunch took place in the Kildare Room of the Westbury Hotel, off Dublin's Grafton Street. There were about ten tables set up, an average of seven people per table.

Those invited were businessmen, accountants, solicitors, engineers, people in the building and property games. The one thing they all had in common was that they had money to spare. They were being panhandled by the party.

At each table, to impress the guests, there was a minister or party dignitary or representative of the Boss. Charlie Haughey's daughter Eimear, for instance, was at one table. Ray Burke, Bertie Ahern, Michael Woods and Fianna Fáil's general secretary Frank Wall were assigned to other tables. Charlie Haughey himself was at one table.

And at the next table, Paul Kavanagh.

Paul Kavanagh was the party bagman, the collector of donations from business interests. It is standard practice within Fianna Fáil, Fine Gael and the PDs to solicit secret funding from business interests. On a systematic basis, wealthy people are invited to occasions such as this, stroked and flattered and "consulted", and later approached for money. They are assured that such donations will be kept secret.

The standard party line from the politicians is that if anyone attaches conditions to a donation it will be returned. This may well be true. The blatant acceptance of a bribe would run against these people's self-image. It would also subtly alter the relationship between the politicians and the businessmen.

It is made quite clear at occasions such as this that the party has the collective interests of the guests at heart. The socialising with ministers might or might not come in handy later on, if one needs to lobby a minister.

It wasn't a particularly leisurely lunch, all concerned had business to attend to. When they had finished their salmon Charlie Haughey stood up to make a speech.

It lasted just two minutes. Everyone knew where Charlie stood, he didn't have to convince this kind of audience that he was on their side. The economy was recovering, he told the businessmen. And he and Fianna Fáil would be willing to listen to any suggestions or ideas their guests might have.

Haughey, of course, did not ask for money. Nothing so crude as a financial transaction would take place here. The businessmen would be approached later. In fact, Haughey made a joke about the reason they had all gathered here. "There is", he said, "such a thing as a free lunch".

Amid applause, Haughey then departed to fulfil another engagement. The businessmen and the party people stayed and chatted.

• *Paul Kavanagh, the party's money man*

The acceptance of large donations from vested interests is obviously questionable. It is even more so given the extraordinary lengths that are gone to in order that the under-the-table funding is kept secret.

As the lunch ended word circulated through the guests that there was a reporter outside the door, watching the entrance to the Kildare Room. Some decided they didn't mind, they would walk out across the lobby and down the stairs to the front exit.

Others went to an emergency exit and left by the back stairs.

Some of those who came out into the lobby left the hotel. Others took the elevator to the fourth floor.

Paul Kavanagh, the party money man, was staying in Room 404.

• *Charlie Haughey at home.*

Charlie's Money

TO SPEAK OPENLY ABOUT CHARLIE Haughey's wealth was considered to be indulging in the politics of begrudgery. There are some things of which one just does not speak in civilised company.

No leader of Fianna Fáil, no leader of any political party, before Charlie Haughey exhibited such wealth. From the late 1960s he lived in a large house, designed by Gandon, on a large estate at Kinsealy, North County Dublin. His house was furnished in the style to which such houses are accustomed. In his younger days Haughey rode to hounds in the manner of a country squire.

Later he bought an island off the west coast and built a house there, airlifting in the materials by helicopter.

What aroused curiosity was not just the fact of such abundant wealth but the source of it. Haughey was an accountant before entering politics and was not a rich man. It was while in public service, as a TD and minister, that he acquired the trappings of wealth.

As always when there is a mystery there is no shortage of explanations proffered, and over the years the speculation about Haughey's wealth provoked many wild theories. For his followers the wealth added to his charisma. For his detractors it was one more reason to be suspicious of him.

• *A man and his Ballagh.*

The Patron

PICTURE THE ARTIST. HE HAS A MINOR reputation, he knows he is good, the living he is making is not quite up to that of the average fuzzy-cheeked supermarket under-manager. He gets a summons. Bring some of your work, give The Boss a look at it.

Among the work there's a drawing of Haughey. It's not too kind to him, if you look at it in a certain light. He points to one drawing, then another, says he'll take those ones. He takes the drawing of himself. By and by he will accumulate an impressive collection of images of himself, kind and unkind.

The artist thanks the patron and leaves. A week or two later he gets a message to come and collect an envelope. In it there's a handful of banknotes.

Sometimes it was not so informal. Artists were commissioned. The Robert Ballagh painting of Haughey hangs above a door in Haughey's home. The painting is of Haughey addressing a cheering crowd at an Ard Fheis. He stands in front of a huge photo of himself, with another photo of himself on the Ard Fheis programme being waved in the foreground.

When Haughey set up Aosdana, which fetes certain artists and provides them with a small but guaranteed income, sceptics wondered what was going on. Was Haughey now, as well as buying the art, trying to buy the artists as well?

For decades, an inward-looking nation had

• *Aosdana, the State's official artists, meet at Dublin Castle.*

treated its artists with contempt. Blessed with writers and actors of international calibre, the nation was among the most censored in Europe. The expansion of the 1960s, the opening up of the country to foreign capital, required an educated workforce. That, and television, softened old attitudes to the artist. Haughey, who fancied himself as a man of the arts, was the foremost politician in giving the arts recognition. He created tax exemptions for artists and he encouraged the creation of Aosdana.

It's true that Aosdana produced a closed circle of "official" artists. It's true that in the tumult of recent years the official artists have been remarkably respectful of the hand that feeds them. But that wasn't Haughey's fault. After decades in which the establishment's attitude to the arts was one of ignorance and suspicion, Haughey consciously aimed at giving artists respectability.

It was cheap, and it did his image no harm. While the artistic elite were looked after in Haughey's era, at ground level the poorest suffered in the area of the arts as they did in the areas of housing, employment and health. During the Haughey era the number of public libraries, traditional centres of learning and culture, was cut by a third. Haughey's final budget, delivered the week before he resigned, drastically slashed the budget for the remaining public libraries.

The Heir

AUGUST 1982, THE BURLINGTON HOTEL, Ógra Fianna Fáil was doing Charlie proud. It was two days after Charlie had led his troops to victory in the Galway East by-election, sweeping through the country, trailing ministers and hacks behind him, pulling Noel Treacy to victory.

Before the night was out the young party hacks would gather around Charlie's table and he would autograph their menus. His hands were calloused and raw from three weeks of shaking Galway hands in the effort to get Noel Treacy into the Dáil. Nine years later Treacy would be one of those who would huddle with Albert Reynolds to plot the overthrow of the leader.

The speaker from Ógra Fianna Fáil was listing Charlie's achievements. The early success as a minister, the reforms and the innovations of the 1960s. And, then, the inevitable gap in the record, skipping over the Arms Crisis and the years out of office in the early 1970s. The jump to the mid-1970s, "A dynamic and impressive Minister for Health and Social Welfare".

Then, the excursion into paranoia: "Sinister forces, possibly originating outside this country, are trying to undermine Fianna Fáil and the Taoiseach!"

The speaker thundered that these evil people should "never underestimate what we, the soldiers of destiny, are made of!" The speaker was Sean Haughey, Charlie's political heir, the Boss's Son, the Chip Off the Old Schmuck.

Although all four of Charlie's children would rally round at election time, only young Sean sought political office. When it came to articulating his political principles he shared the reticence of most budding politicians. There was nothing to distinguish him from countless young men with political aspirations, yet his success was above average.

When the figures were tight after one general election, and young Sean was a few votes short and a re-count might be necessary, the calculators came out. So did John Murray, former Fianna Fáil attorney general, to scrutinise the figures. Should there have been any need for legal advice in the event of argument about a re-count, some of the best legal brains in the country were on hand.

Party elders, people who knew every road and avenue in the constituency better than they knew the liver spots on the backs of their hands, gathered around young Sean to see if they could help his chances.

The party elected him to the Seanad. They nominated him for the Dáil. They made him Lord Mayor of Dublin.

It must have been personally moving for Charlie Haughey that when it was his turn to take on the EC presidency and welcome guests to Dublin his son was Lord Mayor of the city.

Young Sean tried again and again in Dublin North-East to win a Dáil seat, repeatedly being pipped. But, then, his father didn't get into the Dáil until his third attempt.

It was speculated that the Da might pass on the safe Haughey seat in Dublin North-Central to young Sean. With the father out of power, without the clout of years gone by, with the new regime ruthless in its clearout of the appointees of the Haughey era, the extent to which the party would in the future exert itself on behalf of the son can only be guessed at.

• *The heir gets expert advice during an election count.*

• *Former Attorney General John Murray scrutinises young Sean's voting figures at an election count.*

• *January 1982, Reynolds and Wall, the silent service.*

One Leader, One Voice

IT WAS CHARLIE'S FIRST PRESS CONFERENCE of the January 1982 General Election. Charlie in the middle, Albert Reynolds on his right, the party general secretary, Frank Wall, on his left. Behind them, the posters urging one and all to vote Fianna Fáil "For the Future".

There wasn't much for Albert or Frank to do. Albert put his hand on his chin. He nodded as Haughey spoke. He folded his hands on the table, grinned a little, then got serious again. Throughout the press conference he didn't get to say anything, just nod and smile as Charlie spoke.

On the table in front of Albert there was an impressive looking folder. He opened it and closed it a couple of times, closely studying the contents. Perhaps it contained a secret strategy for the election. Probably not. Along the spine of the folder were the words "Jacob's TV Awards".

• *Say yes! Martin O'Donoghue may speak into, but not hold, the microphone.*

A reporter asked an organisational question of Frank Wall. A routine question: how well is the party prepared for the election.

"Well prepared", Frank assured the press.

And, he was asked, was there any question of the party being short of money.

Charlie cut in. "I'll answer that", he said. And that was the end of Frank Wall's participation in the press conference. No one was to speak except Charlie.

As the questions returned time and again to the issue of the economy Haughey became irritated. "I'm not here to be cross-examined!" he snapped.

Which raised the question of what exactly he was here for. The answer being – to get his photo taken. There had to be some event held in order to justify a picture of Charlie on tomorrow's front pages.

RTE's John Bowman cut in: "Mr Haughey, this is a press conference. You *are* here to be cross-examined!"

Another question on the economy came flying in.

"I've answered that question already", snapped Haughey.

"You didn't answer it!" someone snapped back.

Haughey said that too many people were "hypnotised" by the budget deficit. Five times he used the word. Someone suggested that since the figure in question was in the region of a billion pounds perhaps it was right and proper that the government be somewhat hypnotised by such a sum.

But it was time to wrap up the press conference and get down to the serious business. Charlie and Albert stood side by side and held up their thumbs for the photographers.

A FEW DAYS LATER, AT A PRESS CONFERENCE in the Burlington Hotel, eleven frontbenchers lined up at a table, flanking Haughey. Press officer Tony Fitzpatrick briefed the journalists before the action began: "Mr Haughey will be chairing the conference, so please address all questions to him."

There was one microphone available. Charlie had it.

Eventually a question was asked of Dessie O'Malley, who sat two places to Haughey's right. Grudgingly, Haughey passed the microphone up to O'Malley.

Then, before Haughey could retrieve the microphone, O'Malley was asked a tricky one: did he support the building of the airport at Knock.

O'Malley couldn't give the project outright support, given his attitude to fiscal rectitude. But he daren't be seen to disagree with his leader. Tortuously, he mumbled his way through a reply.

". . . and, eh, I feel that, eh . . ."

And as the words seeped out a strange thing began to happen. Charlie Haughey leaned sideways and his hand began to inch along the table towards O'Malley.

"... if we didn't complete the project, eh, that, eh ... "

Now Haughey's hand was just inches from the microphone that O'Malley was holding to his mouth.

" ... the money that's already spent would ..."

Haughey's fingers were reaching for the mike.

" ... would be wasted – in those circumstances." O'Malley finished weakly.

And Haughey's hand whipped the microphone away.

But some reporter was too quick and another question on Knock airport was lobbed up. This time to Martin O'Donoghue, who was sitting between Haughey and O'Malley. Did O'Donoghue agree with Haughey that Knock airport was needed on economic, social and infrastructural grounds?

O'Donoghue didn't, and everyone knew that.

Reluctantly, Haughey allowed O'Donoghue to answer. But he didn't give O'Donoghue the microphone. Instead, he held it under O'Donoghue's chin.

"Well," said O'Donoghue, "the position I would see ..."

And beside him, through clenched teeth, Charlie Haughey hissed, *"Say yes!"*

O'Donoghue blinked, then steadied himself and continued his reply.

"... is that the commitments made by Irish governments should be honoured."

And Haughey hugged the microphone to himself again.

AND AT THE FIRST PRESS CONFERENCE OF the November 1982 general election the Cabinet members lined up behind Haughey. There was a question on proposed legislation

• *One leader, one voice: the other microphones don't work.*

to abolish the notion of illegitimate children. Haughey indicated he would support it.

What about the other Cabinet members?

"Could Padraig Flynn, for instance, please say ...".

"Why don't you let me conduct my press conference?" rapped Haughey. After a bit of argy-bargy the reporter asked, "Mr Haughey, could we have Mr Flynn's answer?"

"I'm answering for Mr Fl ...". Haughey caught himself and replied, "I'm answering for Fianna Fáil."

Behind him the cabinet smiled and nodded, no one smiling or nodding more emphatically than Padraig Flynn.

BY THE TIME OF THE FEBRUARY 1987 general election Charlie was taking no chances. His first press conference of the election was staged as carefully as an Andrew Lloyd Webber musical.

Beethoven was piped into the room as the reporters waited, the music building to a crescendo just before Haughey's entrance.

There was a tricolour beside the stage. There were two tiers of seats on-stage, with benches in front of them. There was room for 24 of Haughey's colleagues on the stage and each place had a place-name. Someone had worked out beforehand exactly where everyone should sit.

As the Beethoven music reached a climax, the two dozen Fianna Fáil TDs were being lined up outside, in two lines of twelve. They were arranged in the same order that their placecards were set out on the benches on the stage.

The music ended. The two lines marched in and filed straight into their seats. Haughey had a lectern to himself, front and centre stage. There were five microphones on the lectern.

Elsewhere on the stage the other TDs had microphones. But they didn't work. Only Haughey's microphones worked.

At another time, in another place, as dissension was heard within the party, Haughey's press agent, P. J. Mara, would joke that "we are having no more nibbling at my leader's bum". There would have to be *uno duce, una voce:* one leader, one voice. From the beginning, with his domination of the microphones, Charlie Haughey had done his best to ensure that that would literally be the case.

• *Homage to Wolfe Tone, Bodenstown graveyard, October 1987.*

• *Soldiers of Destiny, at ease ...*

• *... to attention.*

Garret The Good

COWS WERE VOIDING THEIR BOWELS. Even as Garret FitzGerald stood there, the cows were just opening up and letting go. Inside the shed and outside, the results of this voiding of bowels was all over the ground. The place had been cleaned up and hosed down for Garret's visit, but an army of cleaners couldn't keep up with these cows. The hosing down of the farmyard had just diluted the stuff. To move was to slip and slide on the liquified excrement.

The smell was everywhere. Heavy and thick. The smell seeped into your clothes and hair. The smell brushed against your face as you moved through it. The smell grabbed your nostrils and pulled them wide open and stuck its head right up your nose.

And there in the centre of the cowshed, absorbing the smell and trying hard not to look ridiculous, stood Garret. The cameras clicked.

It was February 1987 and Garret was spending a day in Meath.This is how elections are fought. Party leaders make their way to distant cowsheds and stand and smile for the cameras.

The outgoing Fine Gael TD for the area, John Farrelly, already greying at the temples at 32, carefully slipped and slid forward to stand beside FitzGerald and get his photo taken for the local paper.

Farrelly seemed nervous, and every now and then he clapped his hands and smiled in an almost cheerful way, as if to say, "Isn't this fun!" Every time he clapped his hands the cows reared back in fright. And every time they reared back the fear loosened their bowels even further. And with each extra plop of excrement the smell thickened until it got like you could almost see it.

By now it was as if the air might at any moment solidify with the smell. Everyone, the cows and the politicians and the press might be locked into place like the inhabitants of some ancient village overwhelmed by lava from a nearby volcano.

What would they make of us, if they found us in another age? The Taoiseach of the Gaels, come with the legions of the media to a Meath cowshed, to have his picture taken in the hope that this might encourage the electorate to retain him in power.

• *Garret, up the pole.*

THERE WAS A MYTH THAT GARRET FitzGerald didn't like campaigning. That his academic leanings made him uncomfortable with all that kind of thing. The myth was peddled by pundits who didn't see him out on the road.

As soon as he took over the leadership of Fine Gael, FitzGerald went on the road, visiting every nook and cranny of the dilapidated organisation, recruiting and enthusing a new generation of Fine Gaelers.

With the departure of old Liam Cosgrave, FitzGerald emerged with a revamped product: New Fine Gael, with the added wonder ingredient – liberalism (... up to a point, of course!).

It attracted the progeny of the middle classes, raised on Rock and Roll and Kahlil Gibran, people with Pelican sociology books on the shelf, fans of Dylan (Thomas and Bob), Joplin (Janis and Scott), who thought Vietnam was a bummer, that there was nothing much really wrong with a toke or two from a funny cigarette at a party (but there's nothing like a fine Beaujolais), and that sex is an exquisite experience but best shared with someone you really love, you know.

Garret was blowing the cobwebs off Fine Gael, passing out tee-shirts, the Pepsi Generation meets Mickey Rooney and decides to put on its own political party right here in this barn. We'd like to teach the world to sing, but first let's Help Garret Balance The Books. And if that meant closing a few hospital wards – well, it's a case of omelettes and eggs. Your eggs, our omelette.

And together they made the Great Leap Forward: the quivery-cheeked ex-Majors from Dun Laoghaire, the lads and lasses in (neatly-pressed) denim, the professionals with the well-oiled swingometers that could detect a shifting First Preference at fifty paces.

During election campaigns FitzGerald canvassed as hard as Haughey and far more enthusiastically. Days on end were spent on the road (while Haughey zoomed back and forth in his helicopter), in campaign buses or trains. In his 1981 campaign FitzGerald hired a train, stopping for meetings at stations all around Ireland, loudspeakers carrying his voice to the overflow attendance on the opposite platforms.

By the end of a three-week campaign, having endured thousands of handshakes, the right hands of both men were red and swollen, the skin peeling. In the last few days of a campaign Haughey would nod or wink on greeting acquaintances, and would sometimes offer his left hand. His sore right hand was reserved for handshakes which politically could not be avoided.

FitzGerald always offered his right hand. Even accepting congratulations at Áras an Uachtaráin, having received his seal of office, the election over, nothing more to gain, he would always extend his right hand and when it was vigorously pumped by some ecstatic Fine Gaeler FitzGerald would hardly ever wince at the pain.

• *Fine Gael's election express stops at Carlow, where FitzGerald addresses his troops.*

FitzGerald was Haughey's main political opponent outside Fianna Fáil throughout the 1980s. From his vicious "flawed pedigree" speech in 1979, when Haughey was elected Taoiseach, to his departure as leader of Fine Gael a decade later, to most of the press and in the minds of much of the public he was Haughey's polar opposite, Garret the Good.

By contrast, Charlie Haughey was perceived as being far less intelligent. But far cleverer.

The downside of the "decent man" image was the perception of FitzGerald as a bit of a bumbler. The image was given substance with the collapse of his 1981 government when he tried to impose VAT on children's shoes (he explained that if VAT was left off children's shoes women with small feet might start wearing children's shoes and escape paying VAT).

In September 1981, he would announce that he was launching a "constitutional crusade", to build a pluralist, non-sectarian republic. However, as the Catholic right lobbied for a constitutional amendment on abortion, and as Charlie Haughey insisted that FitzGerald was not to be trusted on the issue, FitzGerald fell into line.

By the end of FitzGerald's period in office, the budget deficit was far higher than ever, unemployment had soared, the constitution was more sectarian than ever. The organisational and political gains made by Fine Gael under FitzGerald evaporated.

Both major parties agreed on reducing state spending in order to reduce the budget deficit. From June to November 1981, and from 1982 to 1987, when in opposition, Haughey resolutely opposed each and every measure FitzGerald's coalition attempted to take. Later, in government, he would impose the same kind of spending restraints, but in opposition he adopted an implacable stance against the measures which he would later deem necessary for the survival of the economy.

After returning to government in 1987 Haughey began implementing the kind of policies he had opposed for the previous five years. When Alan Dukes, the new leader of Fine Gael, adopted the "Tallaght strategy" (which basically meant not opposing any Haughey measures with which Fine Gael agreed) Haughey accepted this as his right.

If FitzGerald's 1979 "flawed pedigree" attack on Haughey was scathing it was replied to in kind. During the November 1982 general election Haughey accused FitzGerald of consorting with a British spy. The green card was used in a manner reminiscent of the 1930s. The electorate was warned that if FitzGerald won the election he would have armed RUC men patrolling the South.

When FitzGerald concluded the Anglo-Irish Agreement in November 1985 Haughey declared it unconstitutional. He deemed it a sell-out of nationalists. Unfortunately, the very clause to which Haughey took most exception had been lifted from a communiqué agreed by Margaret Thatcher and Charles Haughey after they met in 1980. Haughey's opposition to FitzGerald's every move had become so insistent that he ended up condemning his own words.

When Haughey resumed office he immediately began operating the agreement which he had previously declared unconstitutional.

WHEN FINE GAEL LAUNCHED ITS manifesto for the 1989 general election, the first election under the leadership of Alan Dukes, the new leader seemed to have picked up some pointers from Charlie Haughey. Although his entire front bench sat beside him no one except Dukes was allowed answer questions. A spare microphone was taken off the table and left down on the floor behind the Fine Gael leader. Perhaps, mused one reporter, this was in case Mr Dukes chose to speak through an orifice other than his mouth.

Fine Gael had got a lot of mileage out of the 1982 phone-tapping scandal. It was seven years later and they had been in government for most of that time. How come they hadn't brought in guidelines, as promised?

"Because that's an issue that, eh ...", said Dukes. He appeared to be about to explain

• *FitzGerald's successors don't quite see eye to eye.*

why the guidelines had not been brought in.

"The guidelines were brought in", muttered Michael Noonan, sitting two seats away from Dukes.

Peter Barry was sitting between Noonan and Dukes. "Michael says the guidelines were brought in", muttered Peter Barry out of the corner of his mouth.

Dropping his voice to a whisper, Alan Dukes, asked: "The guidelines were brought in?"

Noonan nodded.

Dukes faced front again and in a voice brimming with authority, and with no hint that he had been about to provide a convincing explanation of why the guidelines had not been brought in, he said: "As far as it concerned what we were doing at the time, the guidelines were brought in."

As the years went on, and as Fianna Fáil under Haughey adopted more and more Fine Gael policies, on fiscal rectitude and the North, Fine Gael would remain in the slump in which Garret FitzGerald had left it. Alan Dukes would be dispensed with and John Bruton would take over.

It wouldn't help.

• *Mary Robinson, 1983.*

The Amendment

CHARLIE HAUGHEY WAS THE MOST enthusiastic party leader supporting demands for an abortion referendum in April 1981. A number of Catholic activists, some with links to the Knights of Columbanus and to Opus Dei, had since the late 1970s been arguing that "Ireland stands alone in her fight to defend the Judeo-Christian moral code of sexual behaviour and the sanctity of life".

When the activists coalesced in the Pro Life Amendment Campaign both Haughey and FitzGerald agreed to meet representatives of PLAC within three days of its formation. Once one party agreed to the referendum, with an election pending, the other believed it had to weigh in.

When a vice-president of Fine Gael, Maria Stack, said publicly that in her opinion there were medical circumstances in which abortion might be permissible she was abruptly silenced by Garret FitzGerald.

The passing of the amendment in 1983, said the best-known Knight in the Dáil, Oliver Flanagan, would mean that the "liberal intellectuals will be silenced forever".

Each year, close to five thousand women having abortions in Britain give Irish addresses. Many more stay with relatives and give British addresses. Fear of Catholic activists, and the electoral consequences of having them point a finger, ensured that politicians would ignore that issue. Instead, while leaving the door open to the British abortion clinics, an amendment would be passed which would make Ireland a "shining beacon". The

• *Anti-abortion activists hold a vigil.*

most restrictive possible wording, equating the foetus's life with that of the mother, was drawn up and inserted in the Constitution.

At an anti-amendment meeting in the Mansion House in Dublin Mary Robinson was talking about a pluralist state. A Catholic activist in the audience roared, "What would you know about morals, anyway? You've the morals of a tomcat!"

When a Methodist minister rose to speak the Catholic activist screamed, "The wording should read - Get All The Protestants Out!"

At a meeting in Dublin South, Seamus Brennan said it was difficult to work out the legal technicalities, that no doubt "the technicalities will be fought for many years by the lawyers and medical people, but we shouldn't get bogged down in them".

Change the constitution, argue about it afterwards.

• *Kinnegad.*

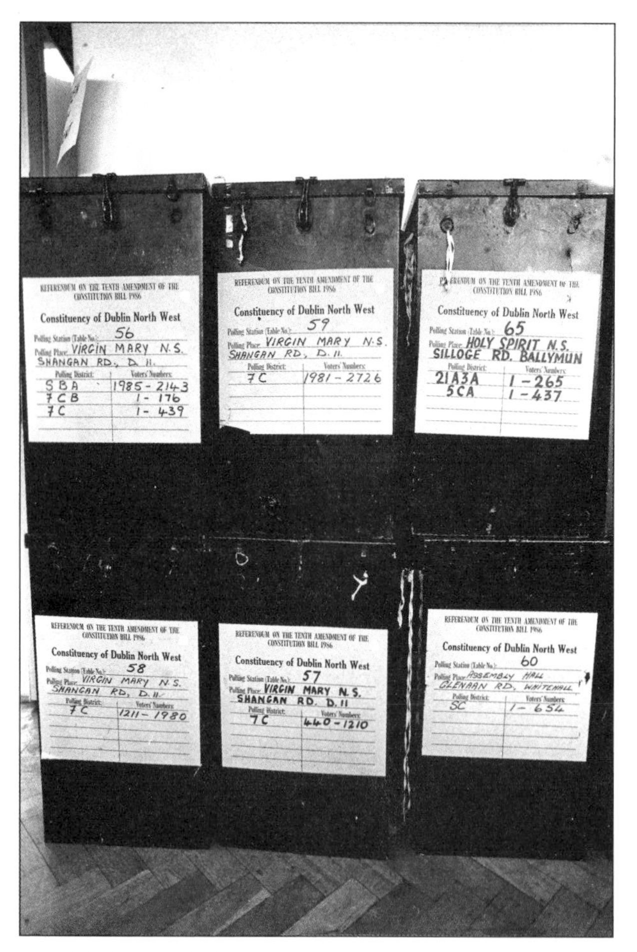

• *Virgin Mary ballot boxes for the divorce referendum.*

June 26, 1986

KINNEGAD, TWO LOCAL WISE-GUYS HANG around the polling station. No, they're not exactly canvassing against divorce. Sure, they don't have to.

"There'll be no divorce here", says one. They know what this is all about. "Garret trying to smooth things for the Unionists, that's what it's all about. Well, Garret is going to get a kick up the arse. And so are the Unionists."

One of the wise-guys smiles. There will be no divorce, here in Kinnegad. "Maybe half a dozen yes votes here", he says. "You could count them on the fingers of one hand."

• *Brian Lenihan with, for once, nothing to say.*

SEVERAL MILES FROM THE SIX-FINGERED hands of Kinnegad, Brian Lenihan stands outside a polling station. Just getting some sun.

Tens of thousands of people are affected by the ban on divorce. It has been the centre of a long political debate. Yet the largest party on the island refuses to take a position. Privately, Fianna Fáil TDs tell of horror stories heard at their clinics. Some of them have their own marital problems. Yes, they say, there is so much pain, something must be done.

But this is politics, Fine Gael will be allowed stew in its own divorce juices. They will be defeated and that is bad for them and good for us. To take a position might get them off the hook.

Which is why Brian Lenihan isn't saying anything one way or another as he cheerfully greets his constituents outside the polling station. "I'm just here to meet my constituents", he says. His presence has nothing to do with the divorce referendum. Here are my people, I am their leader, it is a fine summer day, I must smile at them and shake their hands and otherwise keep my mouth shut.

The sight of one of the most experienced and capable politicians on the island standing outside a polling station on voting day when a major social issue is being decided, and he's smiling, sticking his hands in his pockets, ready to welcome his constituents but with not a political word to say to them, because this is a great way of sticking it to the other crowd, somehow sums up an era.

• *With the Guildford 2; Alias Tom.*

Criminal Justice

WHEN THE GUILDFORD FOUR WERE FINALLY released, after long years in jail for a crime they did not commit, two of them, Paul Hill and Gerard Conlon, came to Dublin. Charlie Haughey welcomed them as heroes. They were wearing whatever pieces of civilian clothing they could cobble together on their release from prison. In a typical flourish of generosity, Charlie Haughey sent them to Alias Tom, a clothes shop where he had an account, and paid for complete outfits for the two.

There was a contradiction here. It was one thing for Haughey to fly to Paris and associate himself with the victory of Stephen Roche, or to fly to Italy to associate himself with the national soccer team's great adventures. It was fantasy of quite a different order to associate himself with those opposing miscarriages of justice.

When the Guildford Four for years proclaimed their innocence successive Irish governments, including Charlie Haughey's, ignored their plight. To associate with their campaign was to risk being declared a Provo fellow traveller. It was only at the end, when the dogs in the street were barking the innocence of the Guildford, Birmingham and Maguire prisoners, that the Irish government gave its support.

When the Birmingham Six were released they expressed some bitterness at this. In the early years of Haughey's reign Irish state

• *Nicky Kelly in handcuffs.*

agents had actively campaigned in the USA to undermine support for the Six.

ON THURSDAY 15 DECEMBER 1983, GARRET FitzGerald's government held a cabinet meeting. One of the issues discussed was the Nicky Kelly case. Kelly was serving 12 years for train robbery and it was widely believed he was innocent. As part of a strategy to persuade Kelly to end a hunger strike, the government had suggested that he sue the state.

Kelly had followed the advice. But the government didn't want Kelly suing the state and winning. That would open up an appalling vista.

So, that 15 December 1983 cabinet meeting decided to enter "estoppel" proceedings to prevent Kelly suing the state. This was a technical device and it was based on a precedent set in the Birmingham Six case, in a notorious judgement by Lord Denning. That evening, Minister for Education Gemma Hussey noted in her diary that the cabinet "had to make some sticky decisions on the Nicky Kelly civil action".

Four months later Kelly was released on "humanitarian grounds". This was a way of getting him out of jail without facing up to the controversy of how he ended up signing a confession in the first place.

The Denning "appalling vista" judgement continued to be relied on by Charlie Haughey's government right through the period in which the government was striking poses of horror at the way in which the Birmingham Six were treated. Three weeks after Haughey resigned, it was announced that a pardon for Kelly was being considered.

• *Frank Cluskey: "I'm next for screwing".*

Labour

CHARLIE HAUGHEY EMERGED FROM RTE'S Studio 1 with a smile on his lips. "I achieved one ambition, anyway", he said. "I kept my cool."

And he had. It was Monday 11 June 1981, and RTE had staged a *Today Tonight* special that was supposed to be an epic grilling of the Fianna Fáil, Fine Gael and Labour Party leaders. Four journalists, Vincent Browne, Paul Tansey, Michael Mills and Bruce Arnold, were lined up to interview the leaders one by one.

Haughey was in the make-up room when Garret FitzGerald arrived. As FitzGerald headed for the same room *Today Tonight* presenter Brian Farrell nervously intervened. "Eh, you may, eh, if you – you may run into your alter ego."

FitzGerald burst out laughing as he turned back. He darted into the toilet, chortling, "The lavatory, the lavatory, anything but - ". He gestured towards the make-up room and left the remark unfinished.

When the programme went live on air Haughey was in ace form. He demolished the journalists and left the other party leaders looking tired. He tossed out statistics selectively, (he switched the international oil crisis from 1979 to 1980 to account for certain of his policy changes) and left the journalists confused and uncertain of how to respond.

Believing that they had been too soft on Haughey the journalists went soft on FitzGerald. The programme was becoming soporific.

As FitzGerald left the studio he bumped into Labour leader Frank Cluskey. Cluskey was very nervous. "I'm next for screwing", he murmured to FitzGerald.

• *Michael O'Leary, party leader, at his last Labour Party annual conference. He joined Fine Gael shortly afterwards.*

By now the journalists were thoroughly demoralised and having let the other two off the hook no one wanted to demolish Cluskey, who was widely regarded as a sincere and committed politician.

Cluskey was so nervous, however, that he assumed he would be pounced on. The first question, from Vincent Browne, was designed as an easy opener, one which would allow Cluskey to outline his party's policies. What, Browne asked, were the fundamental differences between Labour and Fine Gael?

Cluskey, expecting a trap, assuming that the question was designed to drive a wedge between the perspective coalition partners, answered that there were none.

It was a spectacular own goal, and that faint sound in the distance was the despairing wail of weary Labour Party canvassers, all across the country, as they flung their election literature to the ground.

WHEN FRANK CLUSKEY LOST HIS SEAT Labour acquired a new leader. Michael O'Leary was just passing through, on his way to Fine Gael. Having experienced ministerial office in the 1970s and again in 1981, and believing that his presence in office was a good thing for the people, O'Leary had little stomach for Labour's perpetual wrestling with its conscience on the issue of coalition. Towards the end he began to seem somewhat bored by it all.

In February 1982, eight days before the election, O'Leary appeared at a press conference, flanked by civil servants, to announce the setting up of the National Development Corporation.

• *The BO party pose with their banner.*

• *Dick Spring points at the imaginary airplane.*

• *"Put on a brave smile and walk away".*

This had been a promise for years and nothing had been done. Now, in the home straight of the election, two days after Fianna Fáil announced it was providing £200m to fight unemployment, O'Leary popped up to announce that the £200m National Development Corporation was at last a reality.

It was "quite fortuitous", said Mick, that this was being announced during the campaign. It had been planned for months. The five civil servants flanking Mick nodded wisely.

The first half hour went by with easy questions, as the six-page press release was digested. Then the hard questions began, and Mick came apart like someone had unscrewed his navel.

As the questions got more technical and it became apparent that the details simply hadn't been worked out the journalists began to laugh openly. Eventually the civil servants joined in the laughter, as an agitated O'Leary kept insisting that this wasn't just an election promise, it was a real, thought-out initiative.

In the end, even O'Leary himself cracked a smile.

As the press conference ended, bits of the Labour Party were being scraped from the wall. By the next election, ten months later, O'Leary had abandoned Labour for Fine Gael.

DICK SPRING WAS POINTING UP INTO THE sky. Beside him the Lord Mayor of Dublin, Michael O'Halloran, around him various party dignitaries, all looking up at the spot in the sky at which Dick was pointing. The Lord Mayor was humming "Come Fly With Me". The group stared with varying degrees of intensity. Some of them couldn't help smiling.

There was nothing there. Dick was pointing at an empty sky.

The Labour Party arrived out at Dublin airport that June morning in 1985 to launch its local election campaign. This was in the third year of their coalition government with Fine Gael. It was usually Fine Gael which went in for this kind of gimmick, but by 1985 the new austerity dictated that politicians forswear silly gimmicks and stick to the facts. Labour, it seemed, hadn't quite got that message. So, this morning, Labour was going to try to get up there into the seriously trivial league, just like its Fine Gael partner.

The gimmick was a seven-foot high banner that said: "Labour Is Working For You". It would be hauled behind a light Cessna plane, which would trail it aloft above Dublin.

Nothing went right.

The weather was bad and the authorities refused permission to fly the plane over Dublin.

Dick held a press conference. He read out a statement. It included the passage: "There are, perhaps, many promises we have kept that people cannot be expected to know about, because in many cases they concern issues about which we cannot talk too loudly."

At the end of the statement Dick asked for questions. No one had any questions.

After a long embarrassing silence a reporter took pity on Dick and invited him to explain what he meant about having to whisper about certain things.

Dick said he couldn't say anything about that, because that would break cabinet confidentiality. He could not even, it seemed, whisper about it. Being unable to answer the one question asked, Dick brought the press conference to an end.

The politicians posed behind the banner, looking out through the letters of the word

"LABOUR". A daily newspaper photographer with a sense of humour invited the politicians to stand closer to the centre of the word. They did, smiling confidently, not noticing that the two middle letters of Labour are "BO" and they were smiling out from between the letters like they were advertising something you squirt under your arm. It was the photo that appeared in the newspaper next day.

Nothing went right.

The plane's pilot got permission to fly the banner around the airport for the cameras. Before the plane took off, Dick and company posed, pointing up at an imaginary plane, for the benefit of the cameras. "I hope", said Dick, "we're all looking in the same direction".

Twice the plane tried to lift the banner, twice it didn't work. The third time it worked, the banner began to rise behind the plane – then something snapped and "Labour Is Working For You" came fluttering down.

"Put on a brave smile, everyone", said Dick, "and walk away."

One of the party handlers, Colm O'Briain, talked of the 1960s, and how everyone took this kind of thing seriously then and did it properly. O'Briain was wearing flared trousers.

They tried again and up it went, "Labour Is Working For You", proudly streaming behind the Cessna. The plane circled out across the airport and slowly turned around, preparing to fly back towards the cameras. It was a pity, said someone, that it wouldn't be allowed to fly out across the city. "As long as the television camera sees it", said Colm O'Briain, "that's all that matters. Thank God for telephoto lenses."

The plane was too far away for anyone to hear the cable snap. But seconds later they could see "Labour Is Working For You" off in the distance, fluttering to the ground, twisting slowly, slowly in the wind. Dick headed straight for his ministerial Mercedes and was driven away, back to his office, where he could continue running the country.

FROM THE SIMPLE, IF NERVOUS commitment of Frank Cluskey, through the strained days of Michael O'Leary, the Labour Party lurched into and out of coalition. Under Dick Spring, even if he had difficulty keeping the Labour banner aloft, the party began to develop a personality.

As Garret FitzGerald resigned and Fine Gael became ever more faceless, Labour under Dick Spring became more assertive and began to make the running in opposition.

The perennial dilemma remained: go into coalition and in return for putting a compassionate gloss on a right-wing government face the long-term deterioration of the party. Or face the long haul of building the party, and the years out in the cold.

Faced with a dismissive but increasingly scandal-bound Charlie Haughey, flanked by an ineffectual Fine Gael, Dick Spring's parliamentary performances began to impress.

Spring's image had improved somewhat since the 1987 general election, when Dick staged a photo opportunity in Guinness's brewery. Down in the visitors' bar he pulled pints for party and press as the cameras clicked. Glasses had hardly been raised to lips when Spring jumped up and hurried off to the next photo opportunity. Reluctantly putting down their drinks, reporters who had watched the airport banner debacle, hurried in his wake. Some of them shook their heads in wonder at this practical demonstration that the Labour leader could not organise a piss-up in a brewery.

• *December 1986.*

Dessie Can Do It

THE OLD WOUNDS FESTERED. THE HATRED of Haughey simmered and within the old Colley faction of Fianna Fáil there was an irrepressible determination to do him down. Some day, some way.

Haughey went after his enemies. Dessie O'Malley was the strongest of them (George Colley had died in 1983) and when his resentment and sullenness became too much Haughey chopped him off at the knees.

A bad mistake.

Inside the party O'Malley was a nuisance, but one who could be controlled. Outside the party he would achieve a previously unhoped-for position of power. In an era which seemed to have seen the end of overall majorities, where the deciding vote of Tony Gregory or a trio of Workers' Party TDs could make or break a government, sending Dessie O'Malley out into the cold was a bad mistake.

As O'Malley and his new invention, the Progressive Democrats, romped around the country, staging one inaugural rally after another, with people coming out in their thousands, with the PDs clocking up huge numbers in the polls, the prediction that they might take 25 percent of the votes in the next general election didn't seem outlandish.

O'Malley promised a new style, a new integrity. There would be none of the nonsense indulged in by the bigger parties. The PDs were more than just Fianna Fáilers in exile. Moulds would be broken.

TWO WEEKS INTO HIS FIRST GENERAL election, one morning, Dessie O'Malley arrived at Phibsboro Road, in Dublin.

A PD constituency office, run by ex-Fine Gael

• May 1984, Dessie O'Malley leaves Leinster House, with driver Mary Harney, having been expelled from the Fianna Fáil parliamentary party.

• *The PD leader bravely leans on an old colleague.*

• *Looking for votes in the Grand Canal.*

• *Squeezing a sliced pan for the cameras.*

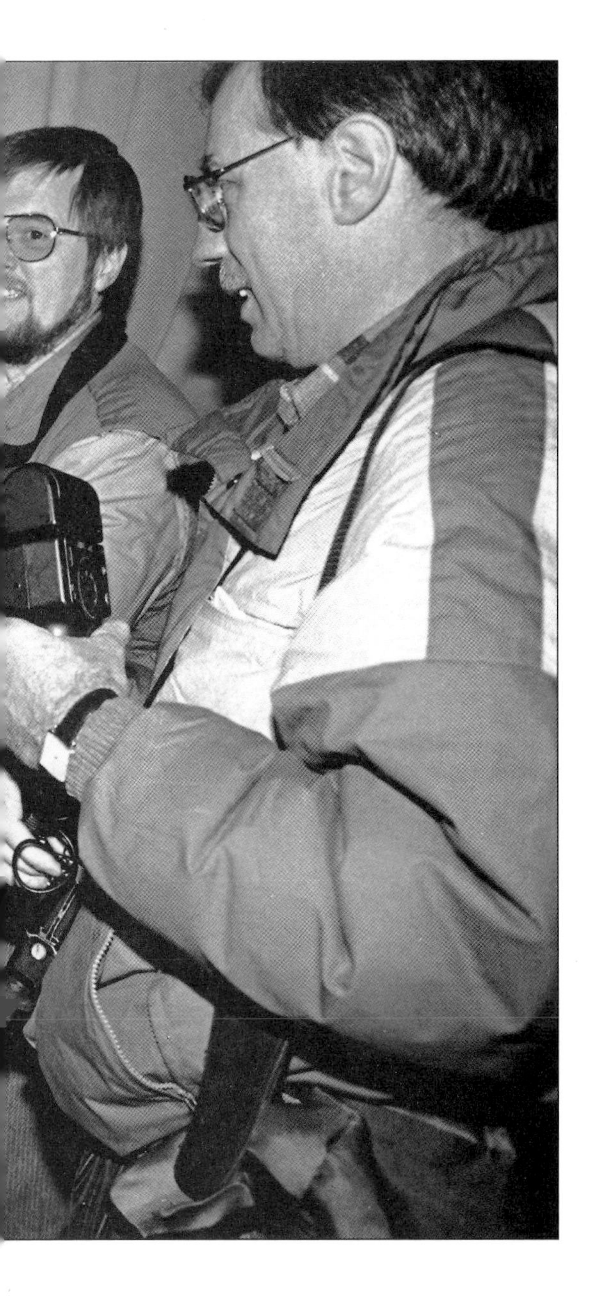

TD Michael Keating, was to be opened with appropriate ceremony. A pack of press photographers was summoned to the scene. Dessie posed for the cameras, cutting a ribbon with a scissors. Except he couldn't get the scissors to cut the ribbon. Maybe it was because he was holding the scissors upside down. But, since the whole thing was for the cameras, it didn't matter whether the ribbon was actually cut or not.

And, anyway, the constituency office had been open and working away for five months.

The whole thing was a set-up. That was the point of the morning's work. Despite the claims for a new kind of politics, the name of the game was to adopt unusual or interesting poses in the hope that the resulting photos would be quirky enough to convince editors to put them in the next day's newspapers.

Dessie moved on down towards the Royal Canal, a neglected amenity where the water is stagnant. He stood looking down into the canal while his picture was taken, his face grim, as though he cared about the polluted water and would do something about it at the first opportunity.

Then he went across the road to a snooker hall and posed with a cue. The genuine snooker players looked on, their faces a mixture of amusement and disbelief.

Dessie left the snooker hall. RTE's *Cursaí* team was outside, asking for an interview. Dessie reluctantly declined, murmuring that he didn't think his Irish was up to it.

While Michael Keating accommodated the TV crew Dessie decided to kill some time by canvassing a nearby factory. It turned out to be a bakery, where they work by night. There was just one man in sight.

Not to worry. Dessie picked up a sliced pan and posed for photos, squeezing the pan like it was an accordion. The cameras clicked.

Then, everyone crowded onto a bus and drove to the Wax Museum, where Dessie posed beside a waxwork of Charlie Haughey. Dessie grinned, the waxwork Charlie stared straight ahead. The cameras clicked. Dessie leaned on Charlie's shoulder. The cameras clicked. It was hard to imagine Charlie Haughey indulging in that kind of thing.

Then Dessie and his entourage climbed back on the bus and drove out to a building site near Lucan. On the way, the bus stopped so that Dessie could be photographed shaking hands with some school children.

In Lucan the site was muddy. Dessie was given wellington boots and a hard hat. He strode around the site having his picture taken. He went into an office and exchanged small talk with members of management. He was then taken to a hut in which half a dozen labourers were eating their sandwiches. The workers smiled and nodded politely as Dessie sat down beside them to have his photo taken.

Dessie's cousin, Pat O'Malley, who would briefly hold a seat in the Dáil, looked around the hut and drawled to no one in particular, "There's no evidence of a Page 3? That's what you usually find in these places."

Dessie didn't appear to be at ease sitting with the labourers. One of the photographers suggested that perhaps he might talk to the workers, to liven up the photos a little. Dessie paused. He didn't know what to say. He was using these people's lunch table to try to get his photo into the papers but he had nothing to say to them.

Finally, as the cameras poised to catch the major politician chatting with the electorate, Dessie thought of something to say. Solemnly, as the cameras clicked, immortalising him in conversation with the working class, Dessie turned to the workers and said, "One two three four five six seven eight nine ten".

O'Malley had the grace to laugh at the absurdity of what was happening.

Dessie left the hut and went over to a mechanical digger for one last photo opportunity. The worker who had been operating the digger climbed down and Dessie climbed up. Dessie posed, hands on the controls, as the cameras clicked. Then, unable to resist the temptation, he pulled a lever. The shovel of the digger reared up and the whole machine shook violently. A flash of terror crossed Dessie's face. Gingerly, he climbed down from the digger and prepared to leave the site, a morning's mould-breaking behind him.

His cousin's voice drawled, "I hope all this mud on my shoes is going to be worthwhile."

IT WAS. THE INITIAL UPSURGE OF THE PDS soon flattened out and the party became just another small outfit with a few local strongholds. But as Charlie Haughey tried, repeatedly in vain, to achieve an overall majority, the size of the PDs didn't matter so much as their ability to make or break a government.

• A flash of terror crossed his face.

• Deep conversation with the working class.

• Geraldine Kennedy TD, victory and champagne at the election count.

The Ard Fheis

IT ALWAYS BEGAN WITH BRIAN LENIHAN. (That, of course, was before it became necessary to dispense with Lenihan in order to keep the PDs happy.) Fifteen minutes before the party leader came out to the rostrum Brian would take centre stage. His speech would build slowly, touching all the bases, nodding at all the old party icons, building and building until the feet of the party faithful were stamping the floor in their fervour.

"This party represents the real Ireland!", Brian would say. "This great party of ours

• *As Lenihan rouses the crowd, Charlie with Frank Wall, awaits his cue ...*

• *... the crowd erupts.*

• *Ard Fheis ecstasy.*

represents anything that is good in the Celtic attitude to life! We want to pass on the torch to the new generation! Fianna Fáil is out there in the vanguard like the Fenians of old!"

He would tell them how wonderful Ireland is. Then he would tell them how the party symbolises and embodies everything that is wonderful about Ireland. Then, with about two minutes to go, Brian would start pumping them up with the stuff about how the party leader embodies everything that is wonderful about the party. The nation, the party and the leader all became one. "This man epitomises everything that is best in this great party of ours!"

And the place would explode with joy and at that precise moment the party leader would walk onstage and begin his presidential address.

CHARLIE ALWAYS ENTERED FROM THE right, that was the rule. Garret came on from the left. Those were the rules for years, worked out with the RTE people. There was no rule about which side the Labour leader entered from.

No one cared.

The modern Ard Fheis is two things: it is a lengthy television advert. And it is an occasion for the party faithful to whoop it up.

In theory it is a great conference at which the party decides policy. But if you ring up Fianna Fáil after an Ard Fheis and ask them for a list of all the resolutions passed, they can't give you one. Oh, they will say, I'm sure someone marked them off on the Clár. But no, we don't have an actual list. And they wonder, with perfect sincerity, why anyone would want such a list.

There is no one in charge of keeping track of the decisions of the party faithful. This doesn't matter, really, as any controversial issues are simply kept off the programme in the first place. The Ard Fheis has nothing to do with policy.

The party faithful get a day or a weekend outing, where they can chant and cheer and drink and enjoy the sheer fellowship of an elite. In such an atmosphere one might even come to think of oneself as embodying the spirit of the nation.

There might be Fianna Fáil umbrellas on sale for £15. A Fianna Fáil tie for £3. You might get to look at a waxwork display of the party's four leaders, courtesy of Senator Donie Cassidy, owner of the Dublin Wax Museum. There they stand at the back of the hall. De Valera looks a bit like himself. Charlie Haughey looks almost like Charlie, except his jaw is too firm. Sean Lemass looks like Walter Pidgeon and Jack Lynch looks like nothing on earth.

Primarily, however, the Ard Fheis exists for the TV cameras.

It's Walter Harrington's show.

Walter is the RTE floor manager who orchestrates the whole thing. RTE supplies the equipment and the talented technicians to allow the parties stage their TV advert. Walter stands below the stage, headphones on, microphone ready. He counts off the minutes and then the seconds, holding up his fingers so that the party general secretary, Frank Wall, can see. Frank organises things onstage

• *Walter indicates four minutes left.*

so that just as Brian Lenihan's speech ends and the crowd explodes Charlie strides onstage.

At home the viewers see only the Ard Fheis fading in and the audience going wild for Charlie.

Charlie does his spirit of the nation speech. "The spirit of this nation must be revived . . ."

As he talks he looks from one side to the other, looking out into the crowd, staring out into the very soul of his race. His speech thunders on with him hardly bothering to glance down at the printed speech on the rostrum in front of him.

He looks like he's making it up as he goes along, speaking from the heart. Actually, he's not looking at the audience at all. A few feet in front of him there are two plates of glass, one

• *Ard Fheis delegates.*

to each side, each set at a 45-degree angle from the floor. They are what he is looking at.

In a cubicle down in front of the stage a woman named Annabella Nolan is operating an auto-cue. This is a long, thin reel of paper on which Charlie's speech is typewritten. The speech unwinds across a TV camera, which sends the words along a wire to two gadgets which project the words straight up into the air. The images of the words pass through each of the plates of glass in front of Haughey and from his angle Charlie can easily read them on the glass. For Charlie, the plates of glass are screens onto which his speech is being projected. From any other angle the speech is invisible and the glass screens just look like two clear plates of glass.

The reason there are two images of the speech is so that Charlie can turn from one to the other as though looking from one side of the crowd to the other. It looks more natural that way.

All parties use the auto-cue today. Conor Cruise O'Brien, in his innocence, once wrote a newspaper article about how Dessie O'Malley had memorised and delivered an Ard Fheis speech without having to consult notes, and about how this showed him to be a politician of great purpose. O'Brien, who left politics before the advent of the auto-cue, didn't know that Dessie had been reading the speech off the plates of glass in front of him.

As the speech nears its end Walter Harrington is gesturing, holding up fingers, indicating the time left. Charlie builds to a big finish, the place explodes again with joy. The applause goes on for minutes, the music starts up and they're all singing "Rise and Follow Charlie".

And as the Ard Fheis ends the party faithful surge forward and begin appropriating souvenirs of the weekend, taking home the plants that decorate the front of the stage, as though taking away a bit of the magic of the occasion.

• *Using the auto-cue.*

• *A souvenir of the Ard Fheis.*

• *His master's voice: an attentive P.J. Mara watches Haughey speak.*

• *Mara whips the microphone away from the "creep with the beard".*

Mara

EVERYTHING WAS CAREFULLY PLANNED. The stage was designed to give Haughey height for the best angle from the TV cameras. The "press conference" in Dublin's Shelbourne Hotel was more of a rally. Microphones were provided for reporters to ask questions. And, of course, could be taken back.

The room was heavily seeded with Fianna Fáil supporters, who would cheer and howl as appropriate. It was the launch of Charlie's 1989 general election manifesto, "The Next Phase".

And *Today Tonight* brought in three unemployed people.

It was a stunt and it didn't go very well. RTE reporter Brendan O'Brien announced the presence of the unemployed men and introduced them: "There's Philip, there's Conleth and there's Larry."

But someone hadn't done their research.

"They're all undecided", said O'Brien, "they don't know which way they're going to vote ...

"Excuse me", said Larry, "I do. I'm voting for Charlie." The party hacks burst into whoops and began applauding. The stunt was collapsing.

"So, I just wondered", continued O'Brien, "if you'd be kind enough to take a question from Philip and Conleth, two people who are out of work for some considerable time ..."

The three unemployed had suddenly become two, with Larry being swiftly removed from the live register.

"This is inappropriate for a press conference", Charlie said, and the party hacks (who somehow were considered appropriate for a press conference) cheered and chorused

"Hear, hear!"

And from one side of the room, livid, came P. J. Mara, Haughey's press agent. He reached in and plucked the microphone away from O'Brien and angrily stalked off, muttering a furious "That's it!"

Arriving by helicopter in Kilkenny the next day Haughey told Paddy Lalor TD that the manifesto launch had gone very well. Except for when "the creep with the beard from RTE" tried to "sabotage" it.

Haughey paused and then amended his remark. "One of the creeps with beards from RTE!"

THEY HATED RTE. IT WASN'T JUST THAT they were fearful of a powerful medium. The Haughey regime saw RTE as an active enemy. The *Today Tonight* stunt was an ill-prepared and disastrous little adventure, but it was a genuine journalistic attempt to bring onto the election stage some representatives of the hundreds of thousands who would be affected by government policies.

What was an entirely appropriate, if poorly handled, journalistic exercise became for Haughey and his people just another example of how the Montrose enemy was conniving to sabotage the Spirit of the Nation.

Fewer ministers were willing to be interviewed on the better current affairs programmes. Tough interviewers such as Olivia O'Leary and Brian Farrell would pursue a point instead of being fobbed off with rehearsed comments. So ministers increasingly simply refused to go forward for interviews.

Questions and Answers, the programme on which guests are exposed to questioning by the public, had to channel its requests for Fianna Fáil representatives through P. J. Mara. Ministers would turn down invitations and Mara would supply some bland backbencher in need of publicity.

In a run of 26 programmes of *Questions and Answers* in 1990, only six ministers appeared on the show, despite constant invitations. In 1991 only two, Bertie Ahern and Michael O'Kennedy, dared to appear. The contrast with the equivalent BBC programme was striking, where government ministers and front benchers never hesitated to take the opportunity to vigorously defend their policies. What, they might have asked, is the point of having policies if one is not prepared to publicly advocate them?

Needing the exposure, but not willing to risk the more serious current affairs shows, ministers increasingly opted for softer interviews on such shows as *Six-One News*, and *Bibi.*

RTE personnel were afraid to say much about this kind of thing on the record. They were afraid of the consequences internally, and of what P.J. Mara might do. Mara, a funny, friendly and sociable type, got on famously with newspaper journalists. Many of them were dependent on him for a daily "feed" of information from sources close to the throne. The attitude to RTE was markedly different.

Eventually, in an extremely clumsy piece of revenge, Haughey's government legislated for new radio stations and another TV channel. RTE's income was artificially held down. It was payback time for the creeps with beards.

It didn't work. Some local radio stations achieved success, but the effort to create national radio and TV alternatives to RTE collapsed in a riot of inefficiency and lack of imagination.

• *April 1990, waiting to welcome Margaret Thatcher to Dublin Castle.*

The Special Relationship

THE THING WAS, ON THE NORTH, HE NEVER quite said what everyone thought he said. Charles Haughey would attract and retain a reputation as a pragmatic politician barely keeping in check a rampant republicanism. Fine Gael and his enemies within his own party swore they got the whiff of cordite from him. The greenish elements in Fianna Fáil nodded and winked and knew in their hearts that Charlie wouldn't let them down. Even Provo supporters saw him as being significantly greener than his contemporaries in the Dáil.

For the British press Charles Hockey (and right up to his resignation some of them couldn't concede him the courtesy of accurately pronouncing his name) was an easy caricature of a dangerous, semi-constitutional nationalist.

In short, Haughey would become, for some, the Great Green Hope. For others, the Terrible Green Demon.

In the end, when allowances are made for very occasional excesses of rhetoric (almost always when he was in opposition) it is hard to note a position taken or a speech made which suggests that Haughey's Northern policy differed in substance from that of his Dáil peers.

Who is this speaking: Padraig Flynn? Neil Blaney? Albert Reynolds? Síle de Valera? Charlie Haughey? Gerry Adams?

"Ireland is one island, one nation, one country, because God made it one."

It's Dessie O'Malley. He was, of course, in opposition at the time. He went on: "That essential unity cannot be put asunder by the anti-national semantics of Conor Cruise O'Brien or Garret FitzGerald." O'Malley, as late as the early 1980s, not only supported Haughey's line that the North is a failed political entity, he also said it was a failed economic entity.

In short, Charles Haughey's political position on the national question is, as it evolved over the years, indistinguishable from that of Dessie O'Malley, Jack Lynch or Garret FitzGerald.

As in so much else, it was his nods and winks that made him different. In 1980 he announced that he was going to raise the Northern conflict "to a new plane". After giving Margaret Thatcher a silver teapot and agreeing some mundane joint studies of the border problem he and his colleagues began hinting that a united Ireland was around the corner. Studying the "totality of the relationships between the people of these islands" meant one thing to Margaret Thatcher and something else to Charlie Haughey.

Even now it isn't clear whether he was just hyping things to give the impression of having achieved a breakthrough or whether he really believed something substantial had been achieved.

At his 1981 Ard Fheis he raised the stakes even further and spoke of "this reunification in freedom and harmony", of a "constructive relationship" with Unionists and a "special relationship" with Britain, of "the solution of an ancient historical problem", of "an Ireland united in peace", of "the ending of the age-old partition problem".

Of course, if you didn't look closely at what he was saying you would end up thinking he was saying whatever you wanted to hear him say. For instance: "A year from this Ard Fheis, if we persevere faithfully, we may begin to see in a clearer light the end of the road on which we have set out."

To some, those who want to hear him say it because it fulfils their hopes (and those who want to hear something that will justify their fear and distaste), that passage means that Haughey is not only promising an end to partition, he's also promising that we'll see the dismantling begin within a year.

Of course, it means nothing of the sort. When you look at what he said and disregard

• *TDs rush to have their copies of the 1984 New Ireland Forum report autographed by Charlie Haughey.*

the rhetoric it means only that a year from now we'll be a year closer to wherever we're going.

Whatever it was, hype or self-deception, it wasn't merely waving the green flag. Haughey, for reasons of idealism or a need to put himself in the history books, genuinely wanted an end to the carnage and the creation of a settlement acceptable to all.

The problem was that, like everyone else, he hadn't the foggiest notion of how to go about doing that, and his hyping of the tiny development of the joint studies infuriated Thatcher. As the decade went on, Haughey danced back and forth and all around the Northern conflict, occasionally using it for electoral purposes, occasionally playing politics with it, but when the dust settled it was obvious that he had done no more good or harm than his predecessors or his contemporaries.

The dominant attitude in the South remained a need to keep the violence from spilling across the border too often. As the years passed, whatever Haughey's private feelings, the need to claim that he was on the verge of an historic breakthrough receded. This might or might not have had anything to do with the May 1989 poll which showed that as an election issue the North mattered to something less than 3% of the electorate in the South.

THE CREATION OF THE MYTH OF Haughey, the Republican Demon, received a

• *Addressing a businessman's meeting in Belfast, April 1990.*

• *Outside, Ian Paisley, Peter Robinson and their followers protest.*

• *Answering questions on his position on extradition, at a press conference, Haughey is closely watched by civil servants from Belfast and Dublin.*

large boost during the Falklands conflict. When the Thatcher war cabinet decided on 2 May 1982 to sink the Argentinian cruiser the General Belgrano, killing 368 sailors and ending any hope of avoiding war over the Falklands, Haughey's government took a difficult stand.

Refusing to take sides; calling for United Nations intervention; abandoning, now that the killing had begun, the economic sanctions which earlier had been applied against Argentina in the hope of bringing about a peaceful solution: these were measures which in other circumstances might have been praised as the actions of a concerned, compassionate and humanitarian politician. In other circumstances one might imagine, for instance, Garret FitzGerald taking such a stance.

Charlie Haughey was promptly buried under an avalanche of criticism. There were two strands to the attacks on him. The first claimed that this was a typical anti-British gesture from the Great Green Hope. The second was fear of the consequences for the Republic of being seen to dare to differ with Thatcher. The economic consequences, in terms of business orders lost, tourists turning away, loss of favours within the EC, were widely speculated upon.

Haughey would indeed earn Thatcher's undying enmity for his refusal to sanction her right to kill the Belgrano sailors. At home, his image as an unreasonable dog in the republican manger was strengthened.

Haughey's position can be contrasted with that of Garret FitzGerald. Six months later FitzGerald would explain his line that even if one disagreed with British actions on a life and death issue one need not openly say so. "There's nothing to be gained for this country in going around expressing anti-British views for their own sake – or in taking public moral positions on a particular issue of that kind when it is not required of us to do so, if it is going to damage our primary interest."

But, of course, Haughey hadn't just been gratuitously taking up a public moral position. It was required of him that he fall in line with the demand that he take sides and justify and support, by the maintenance of economic sanctions, the British killings. And that he refused to do.

Garret FitzGerald didn't like the fact that hundreds of young sailors had been killed, but he believed that maintaining credit with the British was important, for the sake of the North. "It is a question of the prudence one exercises. One can feel what one likes about what British or other governments do – you don't always have to say what you feel if it's not going to be in the interests of your country ... Government is based on moral principles, but it does not mean that at every given moment you have to go around expressing your moral principles regardless of the damage they may do to the interests that you're seeking to pursue on behalf of your country."

Without question, had Charlie Haughey ever expressed such a stance in public it would have been seen as a typical example of pragmatic Haugheyism in which expedience triumphs over principle.

THE EARLY EXAMPLES OF HAUGHEY'S wild optimism that he was making a breakthrough on the North were not repeated. Although, while in opposition between 1982 and 1987, he would denounce the government line on the North at every credible opportunity

• September 1981, shaking hands with Sinn Féin TD Owen Carron, at Haughey's home in Kinsealy.

his own position would, when in government, be indistinguishable from that of Garret FitzGerald.

While in opposition, in September 1981, at his home in Kinsealy, Haughey would pose for photographs with the Sinn Féin MP Owen Carron, successor to Bobby Sands the hunger striker. When in government, Haughey would institute the extradition procedures demanded by the British, who would seek the handing over of Carron on arms charges.

In 1985, in opposition, Haughey declared the Anglo-Irish Agreement, signed by Garret FitzGerald, to be "manifestly contrary to the Constitution".

The Agreement, said Haughey, meant that the Irish government, "accepting British sovereignty over part of Ireland, will involve itself in assisting and advising the British government to rule that part of Ireland more effectively, to help make it more amenable to the authority of the British government".

That was the kind of thing that made a lot of people, supporters and enemies, see in Haughey the stuff that had made him perhaps the last Great Green Hope of Fianna Fáil.

But he never said what they thought he said. And while he declared the Anglo-Irish Agreement unconstitutional he never said he couldn't personally accept it and operate it.

Two years later, on returning to power, Haughey would, without any explanation, quietly continue along the Anglo-Irish path laid out for him by Garret FitzGerald. The "unconstitutional" Anglo-Irish Agreement would have no more loyal supporter.

It was an example of a talent which Haughey would, over the next few years, have to demonstrate with increasing regularity: the talent of being able to come down with equal passion on either side of an issue.

Charlie Haughey's Ireland

• *O'Connell Street, Dublin*

• *At a Council for the Status of Women forum, Haughey faces protests on contraception from delegates. November 1980.*

• *The Knights of Columbanus at Knock.*

• *A Dublin inner-city landlord who has called the bailiffs in to evict a 72-year old man.*

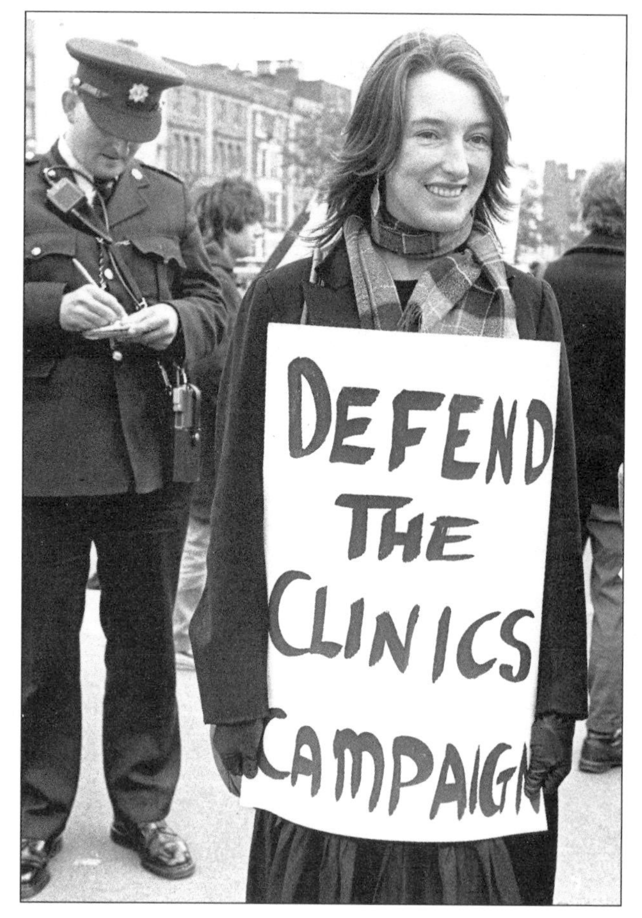

• *The law must take its course, October 1987.*

• *Attending Sunday mass, the Southwest.*

• *Traveller children go to bed in a caravan, Limerick 1989.*

• *Dollymount Strand: Dublin working class youths exercise their horses.*

• *The dole office, Gardiner Street, Dublin, August 1985.*

• *Cashpoint, July 1990.*

• *Belvedere College schoolchildren.*

• *West Belfast, August 1990.*

The Better Way

A MAJOR REASON WHY NO ONE PAID MUCH attention to the politicians when they began shrieking their alarms about the budget deficit was that the politicians lack credibility. That politicians lie and distort the truth is understood and accepted by large sections of the electorate. That they have "pull", that they "stroke", is taken as read.

For instance, when Charlie Haughey's friend Pat O'Connor was not convicted on a charge of double-voting his guilt or innocence wasn't the point. Nor was the point the correctness of the legal procedures which led to his acquittal. What was understood was that a friend of Charlie's got off.

When, on the eve of the Dublin West by-election, workmen turned up to plant trees in an area residents had complained of as an eyesore, everyone understood what was going on. And when, as soon as the voting was over, the workmen came back and dug up the trees and brought them back to the place from which they had been borrowed no one was surprised.

That is how things work.

In the run-up to the 1987 general election Charlie Haughey went in search of a mandate to end the health cuts being imposed by the Fine Gael and Labour coalition. The slogan was coined: "There Is a Better Way".

The slogan was attached to huge posters which condemned the coalition government's record on unemployment and emigration.

• *November 1986.*

HEALTH CUTS HURT THE OLD THE SICK AND THE HANDICAPPED.
THERE IS A BETTER WAY –
Fianna Fáil
The Republican Party

• *At the 1989 general election, Haughey displays evidence of his opponents' health cuts.*

Most infamously, Haughey's posters raged that "Health Cuts Hurt the Old, the Sick and the Handicapped".

Haughey failed, for a fourth time, to win an overall majority, but managed to return to power with a minority government. Although being dependent on Fine Gael support to pass his budgets and stay in power Haughey discovered that there was a silver lining to the cloud of minority government. As long as he implemented the policies to which Fine Gael gave the nod he was safe – and even popular. After mercilessly hounding him in the early 1980s the media now praised Charlie Haughey at every opportunity.

Haughey immediately began slashing health budgets with a fervour Fine Gael had dared not display. Fine Gael in government had been somewhat held in check by Labour, and they had been harassed constantly by a Haughey apparently most distressed at the way in which the old, the sick and the handicapped were being treated.

Free of Labour, supported by Fine Gael, loved by the media, which was delighted to see that Haughey was implementing the policies which they the media, had for years been advocating, Haughey thrived.

Opposition to local government charges could be forgotten; the "unconstitutional" Anglo-Irish Agreement could be operated; the sensitive issue of extradition could be tackled. A bonus was that as Fianna Fáil began implementing policies previously the property of its opponents the PD support began to fade.

It now became clear that the slogan "Health Cuts Hurt the Old, the Sick and the Handicapped" had not been a protest, it was a mere statement of fact. Again, Haughey hadn't said what we thought he said. He never said that he would end the pain caused by health cuts, he was just noting its existence. Whether the old, the sick and the handicapped appreciated that they were now being hurt in a Better Way was a point raised only by sceptics.

IN APRIL 1989, HAUGHEY OVERPLAYED HIS hand. Dozens of haemophiliacs had been infected with the AIDS virus when being treated for their haemophilia. They couldn't get insurance, some couldn't work. The state's medical agencies had infected them and in compensation the haemophiliacs sought an immediate state payment to help them out.

A younger, more compassionate Haughey would have been the first to see their point. They had been infected by the state, they had great needs because of what had happened, the state should meet its obligation.

The new, hard-man Haughey wouldn't budge. There was a Dáil vote and Haughey was defeated. Perhaps annoyed, perhaps feeling humiliated by the need to rely on Fine Gael, perhaps fooled by the polls showing that his popularity had increased, Haughey decided to end his minority government and try again for an overall majority.

It was a mistake. The party organisation's morale was low. Haughey was out of touch with it and with the electorate. Although large sections of the population, the floating pool of Fine Gael and PD support, loved what Haughey was doing, others didn't. While winning new middle class support Haughey was alienating part of Fianna Fáil's old working class base.

In the final week of the campaign Haughey went on RTE radio and admitted that he had misjudged people's feelings on health cuts. "We were not aware – I personally wasn't aware of the full extent of the problems and difficulties and hardships it was causing."

It was an extraordinary admission, for health cuts were precisely the issue on which Haughey had condemned the Fine Gael and Labour coalition just two years earlier. Because of his policies people were sitting in longer queues, waiting months or years for operations that might relieve awful pain or even stave off death. People were dying while on waiting lists and Haughey didn't know anyone felt all that strongly about it. The party lost four seats, dropping to 77, increasing its support in middle class Dublin by 5 percent and losing support by about the same percentage points in working class Dublin.

The election issue for Haughey had been the need for an overall majority in order that single-party government could be provided. During the campaign Fine Gael and the PDs, desperate to persuade voters that there was an alternative to Fianna Fáil, held a joint press conference to launch an "Agreed Agenda for Action". Alan Dukes and Dessie O'Malley shared a platform and said that together they would form a government after the election.

Haughey wasn't impressed. Everyone knew that coalitions don't work.

• *Promising coalition between their parties after the election, Alan Dukes and Dessie O'Malley share a platform.*

A Core Value

IT WAS PADRAIG FLYNN WHO FIRST RAISED the alarm that what he called "a core value" was under threat.

The very phrase, "a core value that we must preserve", was in itself an admission of other betrayals. Some values, it implied, could be tossed aside if expediency demanded, but not this one, not this core value. Not the hallowed Fianna Fáil refusal to even consider the prospect of entering government in coalition with another party. Flynn's phrase was uttered more in hope than in conviction.

Without the general election Haughey's government would probably have survived another couple of years. But the trauma of the election had ensured that it was unacceptable for Fine Gael to simply go back to supporting another minority Haughey government. Alan Dukes demanded a grand coalition between Fianna Fáil and Fine Gael, with equal shares of cabinet seats and the leaders of the parties taking two-year turns at being Taoiseach.

Haughey rejected any such coalition nonsense and sought support from the PDs for a minority Haughey government.

Coalition, said Haughey, would be "a betrayal by us of the electorate who voted for Fianna Fáil on our clearly-stated policy of single-party government".

And again. "Coalitions do not work in our circumstances", said Haughey, "are not satisfactory and have a kind of political paralysis".

And again. "Coalition is completely ruled out", said Haughey.

And again. "I don't believe in coalitions", said Haughey.

And the more Haughey proclaimed his opposition to coalition the more it began to dawn on the party just what it was that Haughey was about.

A limp and despairing attempt at opposition to what was happening came from Padraig Flynn. "All members of the cabinet are unanimous for no coalition", he said.

But it wasn't true.

"The national executive, the parliamentary party and the grass roots have indicated that this is a core value which we must preserve", said Flynn.

But no one really cared what the grass roots had indicated.

The political arithmetic had no respect for the party's core values. And neither, it turned out, did Charlie Haughey's cabinet. The party was learning the painful truth about its myths. It was learning that it wasn't the Spirit of the Nation. That there was nothing precious or indispensable about its principles or its core values. That all the old mystical stuff about the traditions of the Celts and the spirit of the Gaels, about the party being more than a party, about it being a Great National Movement, was fine for an Ard Fheis or a constituency convention but it was really long past time for growing up. When push came to shove there was no great movement, just a political party doing what political parties do: trying to hang onto office.

Power is power. A sub-post office mastership is a sub-post office mastership. A grant is a grant. A stroke is a stroke. Pull is pull. Clout is clout.

And would you ever get up the yard with that old shite about core values.

• *June 1989.*

And as the core value of anti-coalitionism was quietly buried in an unmarked grave not a single Fianna Fáil front bencher resigned. No TD quit the party. There was no wave of resignations from lesser lights. They swallowed their pride and held onto power. And wondered what else they would have to swallow.

• *The Late Late friend.*

The Old Friend Of Thirty Years

THE WOMAN HELD BRIAN LENIHAN'S HAND firmly and looked him in the eye. Her voice brimming with venom, she made an obscene remark about Charles Haughey.

Lenihan was sitting at the front of his campaign bus. It was polling day, 7 November 1990, in the presidential election.

Having started a clear favourite, Lenihan was now beginning to recognise the taste in his mouth as that of defeat. The polls would close in 45 minutes and he had spent the day

rushing from one polling station to the next, touching all the bases, getting in his final handshakes. He was on his way to his 36th polling station of the day and he would make it to another five before the polls closed.

The bus had stopped at a traffic light in Clontarf and the woman recognised Lenihan. She ran over, he opened the window, she held his hand and spat her message of disgust about Lenihan's treatment. Lenihan looked at the woman and just smiled. Moments later the bus pulled away.

Less than two hours earlier Charlie Haughey had been on the bus with Lenihan, accompanying him from one polling station to another when Lenihan entered Haughey's constituency. There was no overt bitterness, but the friendliness one might expect between colleagues of thirty years was absent. Haughey spent about half an hour travelling with Lenihan. He stood in the aisle, halfway down the bus. Lenihan stayed up at the front.

NOT THAT IT MATTERED MUCH ANYMORE, but the controversy started over who phoned or didn't phone President Paddy Hillery at a crucial political moment in 1982. Lenihan was caught saying that he rang Hillery and that he didn't ring Hillery. Now the only thing that mattered about the question of who made a phone call was the fact that Lenihan seemed to have two answers to it. The controversy would cost him the election. It would do more than that.

The whole thing had begun so well, with Lenihan a virtual shoo-in. All he had to do to take the presidency, it seemed, was run for it.

He and his colleagues and cronies had some months earlier featured in an extra-

• *Brian Lenihan at the count centre as the presidential election figures come in.*

ordinary *Late Late Show*, in which they traded anecdotes about such old Fianna Fáil traditions as intimidating gardaí. They told the old one about a bunch of politicians being caught drinking after hours and asking the garda if he wanted a pint or a transfer. One of Lenihan's colleagues told a story in which he referred to nuns as bitches. If some thought such anecdotes funny, others perceived an unmistakable and quite off-putting smell of arrogance.

For anyone else it would have been a disaster. But Lenihan is a genuinely nice man, very much liked even by people who do not like his politics. He had recently escaped death, receiving a liver transplant, and for many his ascension to the presidency seemed just reward for his years of service to his party.

Charlie Haughey came along to the *Late Late Show* to embrace his old friend and colleague. As the campaign began, Lenihan was far ahead of the opposition. Fine Gael almost had to produce a shotgun and start uttering threats before it could get anyone to take on Lenihan. The Mary Robinson campaign had much media support but couldn't match Fianna Fáil's organisation.

WHEN THE BOTTOM FELL OUT OF Lenihan's campaign the consequence for Charlie Haughey was not just that the party might lose the presidency, which by now they felt was theirs by right. The PDs, with whom Fianna Fáil were in coalition, were demanding Lenihan's head. His behaviour offended their standards and they didn't want him in the cabinet. He must resign from the cabinet or they would withdraw from government and force a general election.

And to meet that demand, a demand that a

younger, stronger Haughey might have resisted, Charlie had to behave in a way which would for the rest of his political life alter his relationship with his party.

The worst nightmares of Fianna Fáil traditionalists were coming alive. The core value had been sacrificed. The sight of Dessie O'Malley and Bobby Malloy in ministerial cars that properly belonged to Fianna Fáil had been bitterly accepted. Already there were weak protests about the tail wagging the dog.

And now they wanted Brian Lenihan's head.

Brian wasn't just the party's presidential candidate, he wasn't just Tánaiste, he wasn't just the campaigner who had tirelessly carried the party banner through constituencies up and down the land in by-election after by-electon. He was also the man who year after year had brought the party to its feet at Ard Fheiseanna, roaring its response to his litany of party greatness and echoing his every howl of devotion to the party leader.

He was all that and he was too the man who had fought the last general election from his hospital bed in the Mayo Clinic in the USA and topped the poll. And then came back from his life-saving operation and picked up the party standard and carried it forth into the presidential election.

And now, because of some silly mix-up over a phone call that never mattered much in the first place and didn't matter at all now, the traitor PDs wanted Brian Lenihan's head.

And Charlie Haughey, all the while denying he was doing any such thing, began preparing to give it to them.

ON THURSDAY 30 OCTOBER 1990, AT ABOUT 10am, Brian Lenihan arrived at Charlie Haughey's home in Kinsealy by helicopter. He was there at Haughey's request. When he landed he met a waiting Bertie Ahern, who told him that Haughey wanted his resignation from the cabinet.

Lenihan then went to see Haughey, who outlined his belief that Lenihan should resign. Haughey and his cabinet colleagues had had a meeting the previous evening at which Lenihan's resignation was discussed.

After 20 minutes Haughey had to go to the airport to meet Queen Beatrix of the Netherlands, who was arriving for a state visit. Lenihan left Kinsealy and went to the Dáil, where senior Fianna Fáil colleagues urged him to resign.

Out at the airport Haughey was telling reporters: "I will not be asking for the Tánaiste's resignation from the cabinet. I will not be putting him under any pressure to resign, nor will his cabinet colleagues. It is entirely a matter for my old friend of thirty years."

Haughey, having welcomed Queen Beatrix, went back to Leinster House and resumed trying to coax Lenihan into resigning, offering him various sweeteners. He handed Lenihan a 3-page prepared letter of resignation which Lenihan was supposed to sign. Incredibly, the letter prepared by Haughey and intended to have Lenihan's signature contained the passage: "This decision is mine and mine alone. I have not been subject to pressure from any quarter".

Lenihan wouldn't sign. At a parliamentary party meeting the following afternoon no one challenged Haughey as he announced his intention to obey the PDs and sack Lenihan. No one wanted a general election in those circumstances, so they went along with the sacrifice of Lenihan.

And Charlie Haughey sacked Lenihan, and announced that fact to the Dáil and voted confidence in his own administration, walking through the Dáil lobbies. And as he returned to his seat no one spoke to him. And as he sat in his front bench seat in the Dáil chamber no one sat near him.

Brian Lenihan was sitting at the far end of the same row, accepting a succession of handshakes from commiserating Fianna Fáil TDs, not one of whom had challenged Haughey's decision to sack him.

Although in the end it was a party decision to accept the PD ultimatum, Haughey alone had to take the rap that he had coldly sacrificed his "old friend of thirty years" to guarantee his own political survival.

• *"One of Lenihan's colleagues told a story in which he referred to nuns as bitches."*

The Scandals

WHEN THE FRONT PAGE LEAD STORY OF the *Sunday Independent* 1 September 1991, revealed that Chris Comerford, chief executive of Greencore, was suing colleagues in an effort to prove he had an interest in a company called Talmino, few paid any interest for a day or two. But that was the beginning of the end for Charles Haughey. There was not a sliver of evidence connecting him in any way with the Greencore scandal, but one thing would lead to another and the result would be the creation of a sleazy atmosphere within which the final blow could be delivered to Haughey.

Sunday Independent reporter Sam Smyth had pulled at a thread and before too long whole swatches of public life began unravelling.

Two days later, after a 10-hour boardroom battle, Chris Comerford, was forced to resign and the Greencore scandal was up and running. Fine Gael demanded the recall of the Dáil and an emergency debate, but they were forever moaning about something or other and no one paid much attention.

So far, it was just a business scandal, with no real political backlash. Michael O'Kennedy received a bit of a bashing, with claims that he should have kept a closer eye on the ball. No one could point out exactly how he had been at fault, but O'Kennedy was fun to chase. Besides, it's widely believed in Ireland that it is necessary to call every now and then on some government minister or other to resign.

• *Celtic Helicopters, the company run by Haughey's son, Ciaran, ferries the Taoiseach around Kilkenny in the 1989 general election campaign. The company was to be at the centre of allegations in the 1991 autumn of scandals.*

The government quickly appointed High Court inspectors to investigate Greencore. So far, no problem. But there were whispers of other scandals to come. Another semi-state had been involved in questionable activities, it was said.

By the second weekend in September, on Friday 13, Albert Reynolds was asking Seamus Brennan to examine Telecom Eireann's purchase of the Johnson, Mooney and O'Brien site. Six days later, on Thursday September 19, after discovering that Telecom's chairman Michael Smurfit had an interest in the property company involved in buying and selling the site, Brennan pushed the panic button.

Up to now there had merely been some interesting business practices put in question. They provided material for pub speculation, and they gave the opposition parties something to get angry about. But opposition parties are always angry about something. And despite the growing public unease about what was going on there was no direct involvement by Haughey's regime.

Then, on September 22, Stepaside Sunday, Charlie Haughey changed all that.

NOT SINCE BRIAN LENIHAN CAME UP WITH "mature recollection" had a politician so successfully coined a term intended to be useful, which turned into a phrase of mockery. Haughey stepped forward, the old hand, the steady hand, for a lengthy radio interview in which he would put everything in perspective and restore calm.

"I think", Haughey told RTE's *This Week* programme, "it would be prudent for the chairman of Bord Telecom to step aside from active participation in the board for the time being."

On Séamus Páircéir, chairman of the Custom House Docks Development Authority: "It would be prudent if he were to step aside ... until all these investigations are completed".

The peculiar attempt to create some kind of limbo, into which certain businessmen should step for an unspecified period, and the manner of doing it, without consulting anyone, with no warning to the people involved, was the step which plunged Haughey into political turmoil.

Páircéir in particular was disgusted by the innuendo so casually created. He resigned, as did Smurfit. In a touch of farce, Smurfit called as he left, for the Irish people "not to give up hope".

The farce deepened as Haughey, who had publicly humiliated the two men and called for them to voluntarily enter limbo, announced that he had "learned with regret" of their resignations. Having so ineptly entered the controversy, Haughey found himself hip-deep in it. As the alleged scandals rained down the questions were coming closer and closer to home.

What was Haughey's role in the decision of UCD to buy Carysfort for £8m from a friend of Fianna Fáil who, just seven months earlier, had bought it for £6.5m?

How did it come about that public money had been spent on installing a sewage pipeline across Haughey's land at Kinsealy, greatly enhancing the value of the land?

As the official investigations began gathering evidence, Haughey distanced himself from Dermot Desmond, the businessman whose activities were central to the Johnson, Mooney and O'Brien sale. Although Desmond had attended the then recent wedding of Haughey's son; and although invitations to that event, Haughey had claimed, were limited to close personal friends, Haughey now dis-

• *Charlie Haughey and Dermot Desmond, around whom much controversy would whirl in the 1991 autumn of scandals.*

missed Desmond as a mere "business friend".

Dick Spring asked why the ESB had spent £166,000 on a wind-power experiment which happened to be sited on Haughey's island.

Proinsias de Rossa published a letter written by Dermot Desmond in which Desmond appeared to claim that when acting for a client during the Irish Distillers take-over he had received political favours following "intervention at the highest levels". As a consequence, Desmond was claiming a £2m fee for his efforts.

And when it turned out that Dermot Desmond's company, NCB, had dispatched confidential Aer Lingus information to Celtic Helicopters, a company run by Haughey's son, Ciarán, Haughey's discomfort increased.

On top of all this, the Hamilton beef tribunal had begun its hearings.

All in all, we were beginning to get a fascinating glimpse of the areas where business and politics overlap.

At a six-hour parliamentary party meeting on Wednesday 2 October, four of the younger Fianna Fáil TDs complained that the scandals had tainted the party. It was being openly stated that Haughey should not lead the party into the next election. Not one of the cabinet members, who behind the scenes were jockeying for the best position from which to take over from Haughey, dared to openly say a word against their leader. The silence of the lambs.

On Monday October 14, an Irish Times/MRBI poll found that 77% of the public believed that the government was wholly or partly responsible for falling political standards, and that Haughey's satisfaction rating was down from 52 to 33%.

AS IF ALL THIS WASN'T ENOUGH, HAUGHEY had foolishly allowed the summer to pass without carrying out the required review of his coalition arrangement with the PDs. Although the Dáil had taken its customary three-month holiday the necessary re-negotiation of the agreement was still under way as the Dáil resumed. If agreement could not be reached the government would fall apart.

When the Dáil resumed on Wednesday, October 16 you could smell the rising panic in

• *Haughey welcomes British Prime Minister John Major to government buildings. The Taj Mahaughey was renovated at a cost of £17m.*

the air. It was like someone noticed that the reins had slipped, the whole process was threatening to run out of control, the general election that none of the politicians wanted seemed a real possibil-ity. And a level of hysteria was reached and we saw a legislature absolutely graceless under pressure.

Charlie Haughey made a speech intended to assert his authority and halt the rising panic. But the mood had affected even the man himself. Haughey's speech again and again went off the rails.

First in an attack on John Bruton. Dull, Bruton may be. Not possessed of boundless imagination, perhaps. Deadeningly conservative, certainly. But to charge, in a period of unprecedented revelations of scandals, that "Deputy Bruton is largely responsible for bringing the practice of politics in this country to a new low" was risible, even by Dáil standards.

In his search for a dignified posture from which to look down on the scandals, Haughey said, "I was not in even the remotest way personally involved in any of the events or transactions under investigation." Therefore, it was outrageous to suggest that there was any involvement which justified any questioning of Haughey's behaviour.

Yet everyone knew:

1) – His son, and the company run by his personal friend Dermot Desmond, whom Haughey's government had appointed to a state board, were involved in the Celtic Helicopters scandal.

2) – Despite his denial of Dermot Desmond, the latter was clearly a close personal friend, invited to an intimate family occasion closed to all but close friends.

3) – The same personal friend was now known to have claimed that he was entitled to a £2m fee partly because he was able to call on political favours from Haughey's government.

4) – Haughey intervened in the Carysfort affair.

5) – The value of Haughey's own lands at Kinsealy were greatly increased by the laying of a sewage pipe at public expense in circumstances not yet fully explained.

As yet, there was no official finding that anyone had done anything wrong, let alone Haughey. But his facile dismissal of the questions being raised was exactly the wrong thing to do.

The Dáil erupted as TDs came forth equipped with all the mud, manure and slime they could carry into the chamber. Like a bunch of kids dousing one another with water pistols, they pointed, closed their eyes and let go. Some of the allegations might even have had some substance.

Meanwhile, the Dáil was discussing a motion of confidence in the government. Yet, incredibly, Fianna Fáil and the PDs had not yet reached agreement to continue their coalition. The extent of the farce under way was clear as TDs lined up to declare confidence in a government which was elsewhere furiously trying to cobble together agreed policies – and which might be out of office within hours because of a failure to do so.

The PD nerve held, producing a document which bore all its hallmarks, albeit with many clauses in aspirational format. The Fianna Fáil TDs, relieved not to be heading off towards the electoral doorsteps while the scandal fallout was still raining down, quickly and gratefully rubber-stamped the agreement.

And Albert Reynolds, Bertie Ahern and Mary O'Rourke, still warily circling the threshing, doomed Haughey, could reflect that although none had advanced their claim to the throne, none had been hurt in the fighting. In fact, so absurd were the week's events that they would surely speed the day when Haughey would finally go.

• *Backstage, Haughey waits with his wife Maureen and John Stafford TD to make an entrance at a Cairde Fáil dinner, 28 November 1991.*

An Air of Doom

THEY WERE CIRCLING THE WOUNDED leader. Albert Reynolds, Bertie Ahern, Mary O'Rourke, Michael Woods, even Gerry Collins. Watching him bleed, waiting for the moment to move. It is important, in the subtle protocols of stabbing a leader in the back, not to be seen to be the first to grab for power. He who slays the leader seldom takes the throne. So, the would-be leaders marked time.

Eventually, Sean Power, one of the young TDs who in October had spoken out, put down a motion challenging Haughey's leadership. Albert Reynolds, fearful of being seen to back down, perhaps fearful that if he didn't make his move someone else would, made a grab for power. At a long parliamentary party meeting on November 9 Haughey fought off the challenge, winning the vote by 55 to 22.

He wanted time, he told the party, time to leave with dignity.

He won, but there was an air of doom around the Haughey regime and everyone could smell the decay. Padraig Flynn, Máire Geoghegan Quinn, Michael Smith and Noel Tracey were casualties of the attempted Reynolds coup, losing their government positions along with Reynolds. But they knew they wouldn't have long to wait.

Wounded, Haughey stumbled into another crisis, appointing Jim McDaid as his new Minister for Defence. McDaid had once sworn an affidavit that he had seen a constituent, James Clarke, at a stag party on a certain night. Clarke was a Provo wanted in the North for a crime committed on the night of the stag party. McDaid had done no more than tell the truth.

Fine Gael, angry that Haughey had survived the leadership coup attempt, savaged McDaid. Michael Noonan called him a "Provo fellow traveller". In a vicious speech, Madeleine Taylor-Quinn described McDaid, as well as Haughey, Ray Burke and the new Attorney General, Harry Whelehan, as "untrustworthy". After noting that the above four would comprise the cabinet security committee, she said: "It is an absolute disgrace that a combination of people of such irresponsibility and untrustworthy calibre can sit in such a responsible position".

Taylor-Quinn then suggested that McDaid would leak information to the IRA. "I wonder now, will the terrorist organisations of this country be privy to very secret security matters". All of these sentiments were later endorsed by the Fine Gael leadership.

Taylor-Quinn later withdrew the charge against the Attorney General but left the charges hanging against Haughey, Burke and McDaid.

The PDs made it clear that they wanted McDaid sacked. Everyone knew, and said so, that McDaid had behaved with honesty and integrity, that he was a long-time opponent of the Provos, that he had done nothing wrong. But just as Brian Lenihan had to be sacrificed at the demand of the PDs, so Haughey sacrificed Jim McDaid.

There was ill-concealed glee at Haughey's embarrassment, and the air of doom became more foul.

Still, the would-be leaders hesitated. To make a premature move would be politically fatal. What the game needed was for someone outside all this, someone with nothing to lose, to deliver Haughey a fatal blow.

• Haughey Loyalists outside the marathon Fianna Fáil leadership meeting, 9 November 1991.

MERCURY

And Now The End Is Near

FOR NINE YEARS HE CLUTCHED HIS LITTLE secrets to himself. Now and then he hinted that he might reveal all and scandalize the nation. "I carried the can for the party", he grumbled in 1984, two years after he was dumped by Charlie Haughey. "I've carried the can long enough", he threatened. He wouldn't be the scapegoat any longer.

But it was just hot air and all but the most gullible knew it.

Seven more years passed and Sean Doherty was left out in the cold. When he lost his Dáil seat the party took pity on him and made him Cathaoirleach of the Seanad, where he could huff and puff at David Norris but otherwise do little harm.

Finally, whether as part of a plan to springboard Albert Reynolds into the leadership of the party, or just out of plain bitterness, Sean Doherty erupted. He went on RTE's *Nighthawks* and claimed that when he tapped journalists' phones back in 1982 he did so to protect cabinet security and "people knew what I was doing".

The following week, on January 21, Doherty went all the way, charging that he had, in 1982, given Charlie Haughey transcripts of the tapped phone calls.

AT FIRST, WHAT EVERYONE WONDERED was whether Doherty was telling the truth now or had he been telling the truth in 1983, when he said that Haughey knew nothing of the phone taps. As the days passed the issue of Sean Doherty's credibility mattered less.

• *Sean Doherty, 21 October 1982, photographed shortly after he arranged for a Garda tape recorder to be loaned to Ray McSharry to secretly tape a conversation with Martin O' Donoghue.*

The PDs once again threatened to collapse the government. A stronger Charlie Haughey, one untouched by the shrapnel thrown out over the previous five months by the exploding scandals, might have stood his ground. A Haughey who had not jettisoned Brian Lenihan and Jim McDaid in order to preserve his government, might have had the moral authority to face down the PDs and lead Fianna Fáil into an election.

A Haughey whose political demise had not been openly discussed and taken for granted over the previous few months might have dared to try to pull off one last effort at survival.

But the Haughey of January 1992, bloodied and sneered at, was vulnerable.

Doherty had in effect entered an unspoken alliance of convenience with the PDs, the party which epitomised the values of the Dublin 4 set which Doherty allegedly despised. His voice trembling, he handed them the knife and they knew where to stick it.

The cruel logic which Haughey had applied when dealing with Brian Lenihan and Jim McDaid was now being used on him. His guilt or innocence of the charge thrown at him mattered less than expedience. Right or wrong, a sacrifice was needed to placate the PDs.

It's been nice to know you, Charlie, don't slam the door on your way out.

WHEN SEAN DOHERTY WENT ON *Nighthawks* he donned the martyr's robe which so ill-fits him. For years he had been moaning about how he had to "carry the can" for everyone else. This whine was taken up and given respectability in John Waters's best-selling book, *Jiving at the Crossroads.*

Waters developed the whine into a theory about an urban-rural divide. Doherty could now pose as a victim of Dublin 4's distaste for the "traditional values" of the "real Ireland".

On the *Nighthawks* interview Doherty castigated the supposed Dublin 4 set. "They've left their wives, most of them", he sneered. "They don't practice their religion and they don't want the rest of us to practice it either. They have no interest in most of the traditional values of Irish people."

Although he adopted a fixed grin, there was no humour in Doherty's outburst. He was clearly putting himself forward as a victim of those nasty, atheistic urban wife-swappers who are not real Irish people. And when he said of his enemies, "I care for them – in a special way", you didn't have to be Bruce Arnold or Geraldine Kennedy to be grateful that Doherty would never again have the power he once had.

Whether Doherty, who is as sophisticated as any politician who ever leaned an elbow on the Dáil bar, believed the stuff about the urban wife-swappers is not the point. He now had an ideological justification for his bitterness.

In truth, there are few countries in the world where there is more integration of urban and rural. The real divisions within Ireland are based, as ever, on money and power. There is also a real division between those whose instinct is to tell the truth, and those who are calculating liars.

THERE WAS A DINNER PARTY AT JOHNNY Oppermann's restaurant in Malahide on Tuesday 21 December 1982. It was a Christmas party for the members of the Haughey cabinet which had just left office.

Three days earlier the *Irish Times* had alleged that Haughey's government had tapped the phones of two journalists. On the Sunday, on RTE, Haughey had said he didn't know anything about it, that such phone-tapping would be an abuse of power.

Sometime on the night of the dinner at Johnny Oppermann's the phone-tapping was discussed by Haughey and Doherty. That was the crucial discussion. Both later claimed it to be a brief discussion. Haughey claimed that when he asked about the phone-tapping Doherty said there was nothing to worry about.

On that night Haughey may have said something like: "What the hell is all this about, Sean?" And Doherty might have dismissed the matter.

Or, Doherty may have said something like: "Hey, Boss, how come you said a couple of days back on RTE that you knew nothing about phone-tapping? Sure, didn't I give you the transcripts myself a couple of months ago?" And Haughey may have suggested a cover-up.

A whole month passed before the new Minister for Justice, Michael Noonan, officially revealed the existence of the phone taps. During that time Sean Doherty, if his later version was the truth, had plenty of time to examine his conscience and adopt a position.

When Noonan made his announcement Doherty immediately stated that neither Haughey nor the Cabinet knew of the taps. He was either telling the truth or holding to a line worked out with Haughey after the party that night in Malahide.

If Doherty was lying then and told the truth

• *Charlie Haughey at the press conference to protest his innocence of Doherty's charges. On the table in front of him is an Irish Times open to Doherty's statement, with paragraphs underlined. The notes in front of Haughey refer to the "Christmas Dinner" at Johnny Oppermann's restaurant, and say "Public will have to decide". The final line of the notes, "Done by Doherty", has been crossed out.*

in 1992 why didn't he open up about Haughey putting pressure on him after the party at Johnny Oppermann's? Instead, he merely said that he "felt pressured" into lying.

Doherty's claim that he gave Haughey transcripts of the phone taps, explosive though it was, was remarkably short of detail. In what manner was he "pressured"? Was he "pressured" at all or did he merely "feel pressured" without anything being demanded of him? In

which case his readiness to lie in such circumstances suggests incredible weakness. If he was indeed pressured, wouldn't he have supported his case by giving details of how, when and where he was pressured?

Doherty's allegations lacked any corroboration. Not a file, not a memo, not a diary note. No dates of when he allegedly gave Haughey transcripts, no secretary or clerk or colleague who saw or heard anything, no details at all. While Haughey was prepared to be questioned in detail, Doherty ran from questioning.

Haughey, in a press conference the day after Doherty's allegation, reached in vain for scraps of facts which might support his case. "Where are they now?" he asked, of the transcripts. Wouldn't the people who handled his papers have seen them? No, not really. If he had such transcripts he would hardly give them to his staff.

Isn't it "inconceivable that I would not have discussed such a very serious matter with at least one or two close colleagues?" No, it is not inconceivable that Haughey would have kept such a matter to himself.

He suggested that Ray McSharry might be able to help. McSharry had accompanied Doherty to the meeting in January 1983, when Doherty first admitted the tapping and Haughey exhibited "profound shock".

But, no, McSharry couldn't help. He told reporters that when he arrived at that meeting Doherty was already there and McSharry had his own business with Haughey and no one in his presence said anything about tapped phones.

Haughey could not (and legal principles tell us no one should ever have to) prove himself innocent.

Two men with conflicting stories. Haughey should have been safe, he should have survived on the benefit of the doubt. Almost any other politician just might have. But the problem was bigger than Doherty. Haughey, after a lifetime of weaving and stroking and making enemies, was being dragged under by the weight of the accumulation of knives in his back.

THEY WANTED TO GET HIM BECAUSE OF the Greencore scandal. They wanted to get him because of the Telecom scandal. And the Carysfort scandal. Perhaps the Goodman business. The helicopters scandal. The scandal of the sewage pipe run under his land at Kinsealy, paid for by public money.

Nothing was proven against Haughey, but too many names of his friends, and in one case his relative, popped up in controversial circumstances.

They wanted to get him because he threw away core values and went into coalition. Because he merrily reversed policies which some considered principles.

Some wanted, above all, to get shut of him because they saw him as an electoral liability.

Going back to the Arms Crisis and beyond, through a political lifetime of nods and winks and knives deftly inserted, there were people with reasons to hate him. What mattered in the end is not whether or not he was party to the phone-tapping, or even whether he lied. What undermined him in the end was that – right or wrong – so many people believed him capable of such acts.

And some people remembered a press conference in the last week of the general election campaign of November 1982. Haughey complained that Fine Gael and certain journalists had collaborated in "cold, calculating and vilifying character assassination" of Haughey. He looked meaningfully towards journalist Bruce Arnold and he reached for a file on the table before him.

Then he stopped and took nothing from the file.

Perhaps there was in the file some newspaper report which Arnold had written and with which Haughey took issue. Perhaps there was something else.

• *Leaving Leinster House, 30 January 1992, after announcing he would resign.*

• *Albert Reynolds at Fianna Fáil election headquarters in Longford, November 1982.*

Albert Emerges

BACK IN 1987 RAY BURKE TOLD THE PDs where to get off. "Nobody will decide on the leadership of Fianna Fáil except Fianna Fáil and our leader is Charles J. Haughey. Let nobody outside Fianna Fáil have any feelings that since they've left the party they can

influence our leadership. They tried that when they were on the inside and they're not going to do it from the outside."

But that was once upon a time, very long ago. By 1992 Charlie Haughey had, albeit driven to it by force of circumstance, stripped away much of the mysticism that had surrounded Fianna Fáil. This was the party that brought waxwork figures of its former leaders to its Ard Fheis. This was the Great National Movement, the Spirit of the Nation. People really believed that they were part of a great movement with loyalty to things greater than its own hold on power.

The things Charlie Haughey had to do to stay in power made a nonsense of the myths in which the party had dressed itself. One by one the core values had been dismissed. Even the final core value, that outsiders could not influence the party's choice of leader, was lost. The PDs ruthlessly wielded the knife Sean Doherty handed them.

By the time the PDs finally got to dismiss Charlie Haughey from the leadership of Fianna Fáil they had reason not to. They had found him easy to work with, a most amenable coalition partner. It was with a certain regret that they got rid of him, but in the circumstances, after fighting and despising him for so long, they couldn't resist killing him off when they got the chance.

ONE OF THE FIRST ACTS OF ALBERT Reynolds as leader of Fianna Fáil was to make arrangements for a photographer from *"Hello!"*, the glossy chronicle of the lives of royalty, fashion and show business celebrities, to come to his Dublin 4 home for a photo session.

To accommodate the magazine, Reynolds took time off from his preparations for choosing his first cabinet. Some might pour scorn on the "country and western Taoiseach" but Reynolds knows that his heart belongs to Dublin 4.

Reynolds made his money in ballrooms and petfood. He was a businessman who in 1977 decided the country needed his business acumen. The slogan for his first Dáil election was, "To Get Things Done, Vote Reynolds One". He was one of the plotters who prepared the ground for Charlie Haughey's ascent to the leadership and was rewarded with ministerial office.

While publicly prepared to work with Haughey in coalition after 1989, Reynolds was privately weaving himself a rebellious image among the party faithful, by denouncing the "temporary little arrangement" with the PDs. His groundwork was so well done that when Haughey finally got the push Reynolds was clearly in front as the leadership contender.

After his election he said, "I have no favours to pay", when choosing a cabinet. He then ruthlessly chopped Haughey loyalists and installed his own supporters, promoting 14 of the 22 TDs who had voted for him in the abortive coup three months earlier. Five others who showed him loyalty were also promoted. Reynolds commented on this in a phrase rarely before heard in Irish politics: "A man's got to do what a man's got to do".

Reynolds was capable and efficient as a minister but after 15 years in the Dáil his views on most of the major issues of the day were left unspoken. He contributed nothing to the debates on such major issues as the abortion referendum, contraception legislation, the Anglo-Irish Agreement and divorce.

In at least one respect Albert Reynolds follows very much in the Haughey tradition. On the issue of privatisation Reynolds once forthrightly declared that Fine Gael and the PDs could talk all they want but it wasn't going to happen.

"We don't believe that assets built up over the years should be sold off cheap to make a fast buck. These commercial semi-states are resources that belong to the taxpayer. If they were sold now they would have to be sold cheaply because they haven't reached their potential." That was in February 1987, just months before Reynolds went back into office and began implementing his privatisation policy.

In short, although he would present himself as a new and different leader, Reynolds was stamped with the hallmark of the Haughey era: the ability to come down passionately on either side of an issue.

THE FAREWELL TRIBUTES PAID IN THE Dáil to Charlie Haughey lacked spirit. That from Dessie O'Malley was probably the most generous and heartfelt.

Perhaps conscious of the fact that those still loyal to him lacked the facility to coin a suitable phrase, Haughey, in his last days as Taoiseach, came to the Dáil chamber equipped with his own literary quotes with which to mark his departure. "The heavens blaze forth the death of princes", he told the Dáil. He quoted Othello. He talked of returning his sword to its scabbard.

"If I were to seek any accolade as I leave office, it would simply be: He served the people, all the people, to the best of his ability."

When it came time to elect the new Taoiseach, Charlie Haughey proposed Albert Reynolds and a vote was called. Haughey left his Taoiseach's seat and walked up the steps of the Dáil chamber and through the lobby, and turned left to walk back down to his seat. And stopped. Already seated in the Taoiseach's seat, before the votes had even been totted up, was Albert Reynolds. Haughey had nowhere to sit. He looked around and spotted an empty seat and asked a backbench TD if it would be alright if he squeezed in there.

• *The touch of power. Albert Reynolds, minutes after being elected leader of Fianna Fáil, 6 February 1992.*

The Balance Sheet

IT WILL TAKE TIME AND PERSPECTIVE before there can be a full summing up of the Haughey era. But the facts and figures are fairly clear.

The year he became Taoiseach, 1979, unemployment was 89,000, and it rose to 122,000 in his first year on the job. On the day that Albert Reynolds was elected leader of Fianna Fáil, Thursday 6 February 1992, Haughey's last day as leader of the party, the latest unemployment figures were released. They showed that at 276,700, unemployment was at its highest in the history of the state.

And the unemployment figures would have been vastly higher had not around 40,000 people per year emigrated during the final years of the Haughey era.

The week of the leadership change was the week in which an RUC man ran amok and killed three people at a Sinn Féin office, before killing himself. The following day, loyalists shot dead five Catholics in a bookie shop. A week or so earlier the IRA had blown up and killed, at Teebane, eight workers who had ignored threats against those repairing RUC property.

Haughey, no more than any other individual, could not be blamed for the continuing horror, but it was he who in 1980 named peace in the North as his first political priority. The days when he was hinting that a united Ireland was around the corner seem to belong to another, vastly more naive, age.

On Monday 10 January 1992 Charlie Haughey went to Áras an Uachtaráin to formally resign as Taoiseach. That was the day that Mr Justice Declan Costello heard arguments in the case in which he would order

• *Fianna Fáil posters in the run-up to the 1987 general election.*

• *Dublin protest rally during the abortion controversy, 22 February 1992.*

that a 14-year-old rape victim be prevented from going to England for an abortion.

Haughey had coined the term "An Irish solution to an Irish problem" and that had been his method of operation. Speak in grandiose terms of great movements and national spirit. Never say exactly what you stand for, never take a principled position, move forward sideways, move back when you have to, duck, weave, manoeuvre. It was a political method that had many admirers. He got things done, they said. He was a survivor, they said. He produced ludicrous family planning legislation, but only he could get any such legislation through. Look at the mess Fine Gael made of it.

To oppose the rampant Catholicism which made a religious document of the Constitution would have been politically dangerous. It would have risked the other policies which Haughey wished to implement. Therefore, you duck and weave and fight another day.

It is a point of view. But no great policy on the North was carried through; emigration drained the young; unemployment raged; and the willingness to bow the knee to religious fundamentalists deprived the nation of rational laws on contraception, abortion and divorce. And eventually, inevitably, horror was piled on horror for a 14-year-old.

Haughey was innovative and imaginative as a minister in the 1960s. He brought in free travel for the aged, and the Succession Bill, which gave women rights to the family home, he provided separate accommodation for young offenders.

As Taoiseach he reduced the current budget deficit, which in earlier periods he had driven up. In the end, what was the surviving all about? What was it all for?

Haughey's single most important contribution to Irish politics may have been an unwitting one. Having tried and failed five times to win an overall Dáil majority for Fianna Fáil; having lost the party's hold on the presidency for the first time in the history of the state; having shredded the unthinking traditions of loyalty to tribal "core values", Haughey left behind him a battered but more realistic party.

Some whooped and yelled when Albert Reynolds became Taoiseach, and Mary O'Rourke declared him to be the "King of Ireland", but that kind of talk had had its day. Everyone knew that Albert is just an ambitious politician who won the top job.

Up to Haughey's time the party could claim that it embodied a unique set of traditions, that it represented the Spirit of the Nation. And it could insist that loyalty to the nation demanded loyalty to the party. To oppose the party was to be somehow un-Irish.

At the end of the Haughey era the party was a step closer to acknowledging that in a complex society no single body can claim to represent within itself all the different interests of that society. The Haughey era was a bridge between the days of de Valera and Lemass, when the party genuinely saw itself as a national movement, and the post-Haughey era, when such delusions could not be sustained.

Less than three weeks after Haughey left office the Commission on the Aims and Structures of Fianna Fáil presented its report. It urged a recruiting drive to ease the £2.3m debt which the party had built up through profligate spending on elections and Ard Fheiseanna. To attract members, a personalised membership card was proposed. The holder of the card would be entitled to "a very attractive package of discounts" when purchasing from "selected retail outlets".

The party's self-image of Soldiers of Destiny no longer rang true. Post-Haughey, the party would feel more comfortable with an image of itself setting forth with its personalised membership and discount cards, the Shoppers of Destiny. The new image might not be as grandiose as the old one but it peddled fewer illusions.

• *Albert Reynolds' first Ard Fheis as leader, 7 March 1992.*